DATE DUE

14			
14			
10			
13			
NOV			
NOV 26 1987			
13			
14			
17			

COLOR CRAFTS

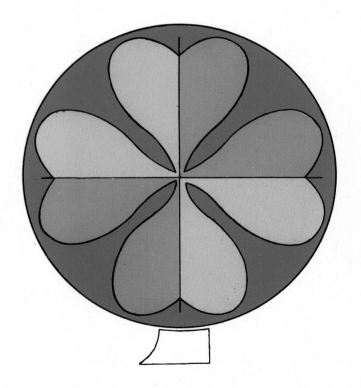

Franklin Watts, Inc.

Other titles in the Color Crafts
series already published are:

Working with paper

Card and cardboard

String, raffia and material

Wire, wood and cork

Painting, printing and modeling

Needlework, macramé and knitting

Papier mâché, dyeing and leatherwork

Working with odds and ends

© 1974 by Ediciones ALTEA
General Mola, 84. Madrid-6
PRINTED IN SPAIN
LITOPRINT, S. A.—Fuenlabrada (MADRID)
Depósito legal: M. 29.895 - 1974
First published June 1973
First English edition 1975
First American publication 1975 by Franklin Watts, Inc.
© 1973 by Ediciones Altea
English translation © 1974 Macdonald & Co. (Publishers) Ltd.
St Giles House, 49/50 Poland Street, London W1A 2LG

Printed in Spain

Library of Congress Catalog Card Number 74-18747

ISBN: 531-02805-4

Volume 9

Working from nature

The projects in this book are divided into five grades, from very simple to advanced. The color key below shows the grades and corresponding symbols, which are repeated at the beginning of each project for easy reference. The very simple projects are designed for younger children but the grades are only intended as a rough guide. Very young children may need some help.

 Very simple

 Easy

 Moderately easy

 More complex

 Advanced

Working from Nature is the ninth volume in the *Color Crafts* series. It shows how the materials that you can collect during a walk in the countryside, in a park or on the beach can be transformed into attractive games, animals, and figures. All the projects are illustrated with step-by-step color pictures and photographs of the finished works.

The projects are designed to show how materials can be used—it is not important to copy the projects exactly. Once the basic techniques have been learned you can experiment with ideas of your own.

Where the text suggests using glue to stick different materials together, we suggest the use of PVA glue, or any strong impact adhesive. Quite often the projects require a clear varnish; this is easily made by mixing some PVA glue with an equal amount of water. If you need to use a sharp knife, we suggest one of the throw-away blade types. The best all-purpose paints for the materials in this book are Polymer or Acrylic paints.

The color-coded square at the beginning of each project tells you how difficult each one is. If you get stuck on a project you can turn to an earlier one and go back to the harder one later.

SEED NECKLACE

Pierce the seeds while they are still soft. This can be done in one of two ways: either with the needle as they are threaded onto the necklace, or else beforehand with a fine bradawl. Using a bradawl is better, since it avoids the risk of the needle breaking. The thread can be doubled up for greater strength.

The seeds should be threaded according to a pattern: ten small seeds followed by a large one, for example.

To make the loops in the necklace, pass the thread a second time through one of the large seeds, as shown in the drawing, then continue threading on the seeds.

When the work is finished, tie the thread in a tight double knot, so that there is no chance of its coming undone.

This kind of necklace can also be made with other materials: sunflower seeds, dried peas or peanut shells, for example.

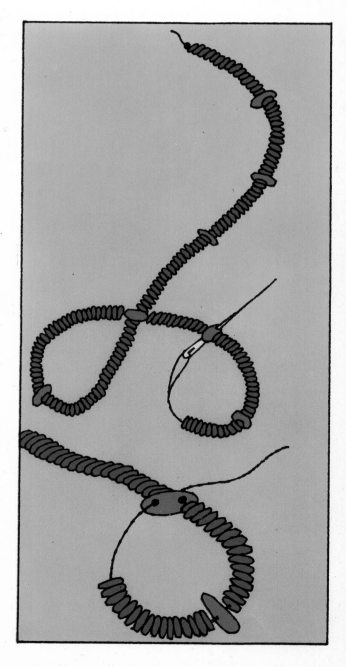

ANIMALS

Collect some smooth stones of different shapes. Try to 'see' the shape enclosed in each stone. The stone may suggest the shape of an animal. Try to bring out the shape with a few strokes of the paintbrush.

The maggot has been made by painting the body, eyes and mouth.

The eyes and beak were enough to suggest a pigeon.

For the piglet, the outline of the head and the mouth were enough to bring out the animal's character.

The tiger's head is more complicated. It has mouth, whiskers and nose. The eyes are squinting, giving the animal a mischievous expression as it crouches on the back of the elephant.

The elephant is made by painting in the ears and eyes. You can give the trunk a few wrinkles to make it more lifelike.

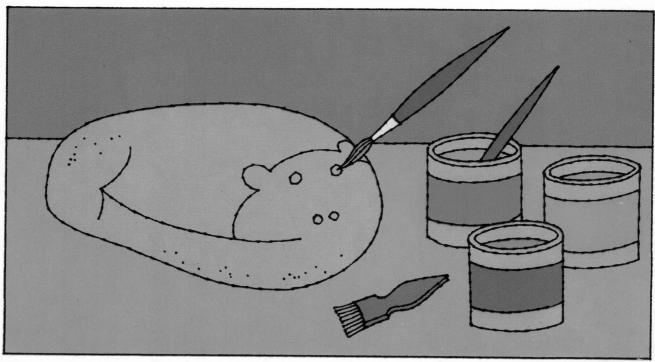

These stone animals can be used as paperweights, or simply as ornaments on a shelf.

DUCK, TORTOISE AND LIZARD

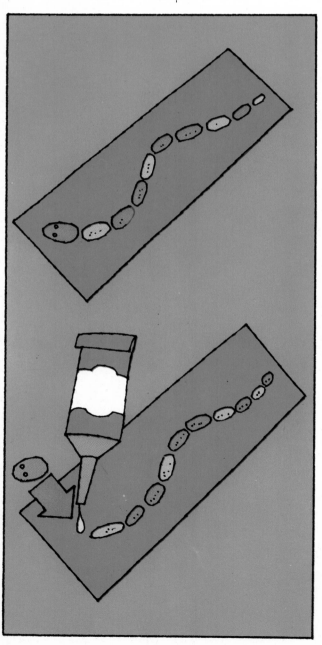

Porous stones are stones that absorb water. Porous stones are sometimes strangely shaped. They often have holes in them and are very useful for making heads. The holes can be made to look like eyes.

Find stones that suggest animals' heads; a duck or a tortoise, for example. Make the rest of each animal's body with pebbles or more pieces of porous stone.

The stones can be arranged on a piece of cardboard, and then stuck down with a drop of glue. Take care not to use too much glue. It may stain the cardboard or form a ring around the edge of the stones.

When it is finished, the picture can be framed or simply pinned to the wall with drawing pins.

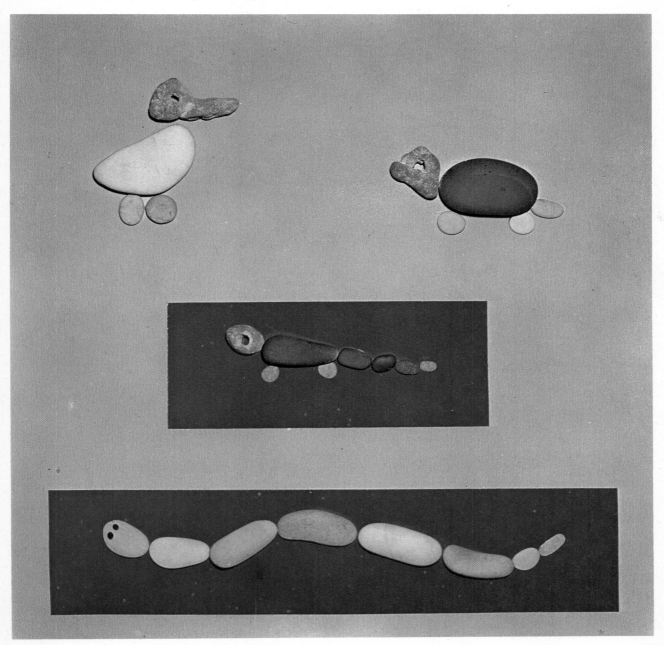

MATERIALS:
● Mussel shells
● Smaller shells
● Pebbles
● PVA glue
● Colored card

BUTTERFLY

Arrange the different parts of the butterfly on the card. Choose a brightly colored card so that the butterfly stands out well.

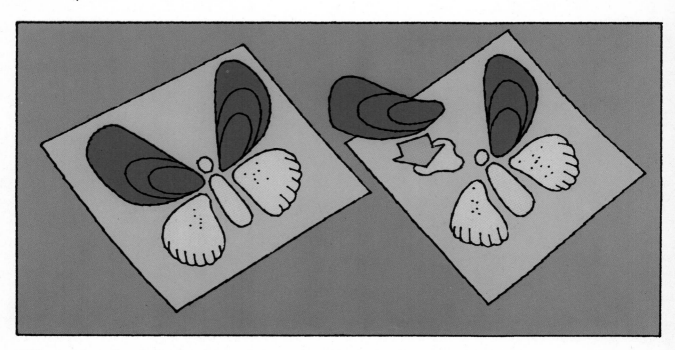

When the final design has been decided upon, the different pieces can be stuck down on the card. Place a drop of glue on the card for each piece, and then press the shell or pebble firmly in position.

Be careful not to use too much glue, so as to avoid staining the card around the figure.

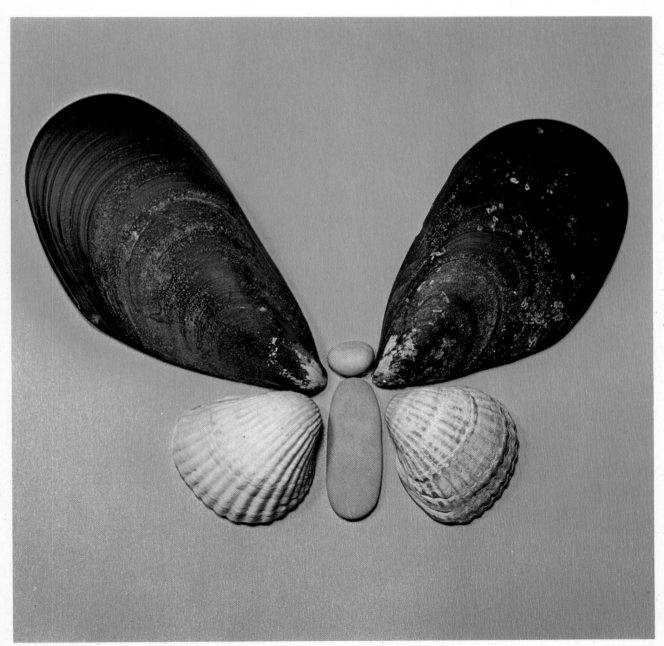

KEY RING

Stones of this type can often be found on beaches. The constant movement of the water wears holes in them. These stones make good key rings.

Thread a few strands of colored thread through the hole. Divide the strands into three equal parts, and then braid them together. Knot the braided thread together at the ends.

The key is attached to the end of the braided thread as shown in the drawing.
The key can easily be detached from the thread, and you can add another one if you like.

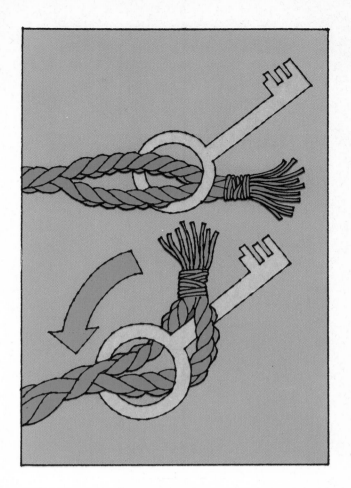

MATERIALS:
- A porous stone with holes in it
- Pieces of colored leather
- Enamel paint

PENDANT

Choose an attractively shaped stone with a hole at one side, so that it will hang well on the cord. The stone is then painted. Paint one side first and leave it to dry, then turn the stone over and paint the other side.

To make the cord, take the pieces of leather and round off the corners. Then cut a narrow strip around the edge of each piece. Continue in a spiral until you have a piece of the desired length.

It does not matter if the strips are not perfectly straight. In order to obtain perfectly straight strips, you would have to cut them from very large pieces of leather.

Braid the strips together, following the picture above. Braid them neatly, stretching each strip slightly to make it follow the shape of the cord.
The leather is flexible and can easily be pulled into shape.
The finished cord is then passed through the hole in the stone and the ends are tied in a knot.

PICK UP STICKS

The best sticks for this project are sticks of thin cane. If you cannot find cane of this sort, ordinary sticks or straws will do. Make sure that all the sticks are the same length.

If the cane is a little rough around the knots, smooth these down with sandpaper. The ends should be cut as cleanly as possible. Pull off any loose splinters and smooth the edges with sandpaper.

Once prepared, the sticks are ready for painting. Use about 25 or 35 of them and divide them into several equal groups. Paint each group a different color. In the game shown here, there are 7 green sticks, 7 blue, 7 yellow, 6 red and 1 black. Leave the sticks to dry and you are ready to play.

To start the game, gather the colored sticks in a bunch around the black one, which is the king. Hold them upright on the table. Then open your hand and let them fall freely.

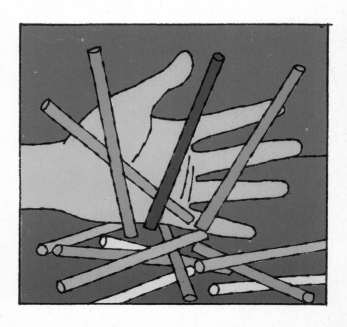

Each player tries to remove the sticks one by one from the heap without moving any of the others.
If he moves one of the other sticks, he gives up his turn to the next player.
Each stick which is removed scores a number of points for the player who removes it.
The black stick scores 10 points, and is the only one which can be used to help remove other sticks.
The red sticks score 8 points each, the green 5 points, the yellow 3 points and the blue 1 point.
The player with the highest number of points at the end of the game is the winner.

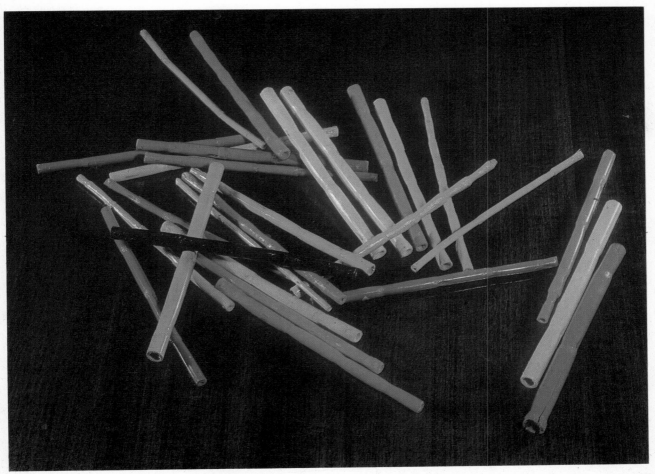

VILLAGE

The flat-sided stones should be painted to look like houses, with windows, doors and roofs.
The door and window frames should be painted the same color so that they stand out more strongly.
A stone with two sides shaped like a steep roof can be painted with a red crisscross pattern to suggest tiles.

The trees are made in two parts: one stone shaped like a column for the trunk and a round one for the top. Join the two pieces together with plenty of glue.

When the glue is dry, the tree can be painted, as shown in the photograph. It is best to paint the top first and leave the paint to dry before painting the trunk.

MATERIALS:
- ● **Flat stones**
- ● **Gloss or matt paints**
- ● **Special safety pins for brooches**
- ● **PVA glue**

BROOCHES

Wash the stones thoroughly to remove dust and mud.
When they are completely dry, draw in the outlines of the decoration with a pencil.

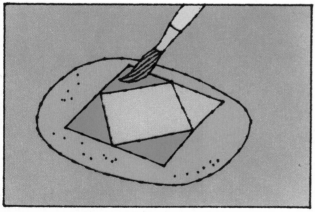

Paint the designs with matt or gloss paint. You can also combine matt and gloss colors on the same stone to give a more varied effect.

When the paint is completely dry, stick the safety pins to the underside of the brooches. The join between the two must be very strong; use plenty of glue and reinforce places where they do not join perfectly with new coats of glue.

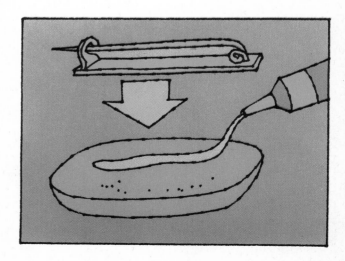

Make sure that the glue is completely
dry before you wear the brooches.

PREHISTORIC MONUMENTS

The men of prehistoric times raised stone monuments. These were enormous blocks which they arranged in a special manner. This project shows how to make three kinds of prehistoric monument; menhirs, dolmens and cromlechs.

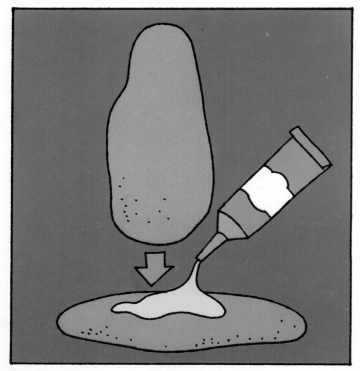

Menhirs are tall blocks fastened firmly in the ground. Menhirs usually taper away at the top. Glue the menhir on a flat stone base.

Support the menhir with books while it dries.

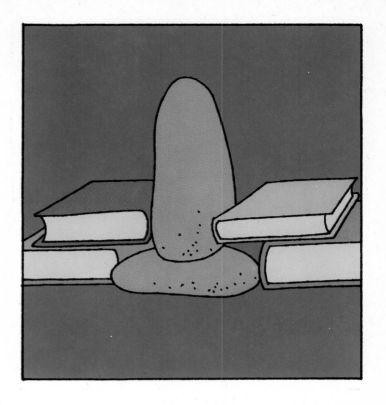

The dolmen is formed by two upright rocks supporting a third one in the form of a roof. Glue the rocks, one by one, to their base. The cromlech consists of enormous stone slabs fixed in the ground and arranged in a circle. Other, equally gigantic stones are supported on top of them.

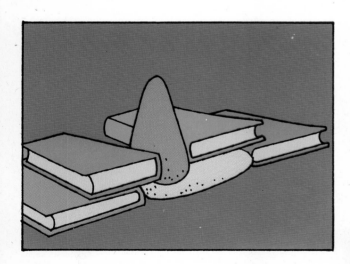

Support the dolmens and cromlechs with books while they dry. Varnish the stones.

To make the varnish, mix some glue with an equal amount of water. The varnish brings out the color of the stone.

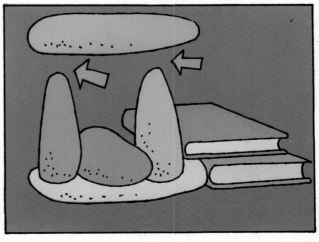

27

The cromlech shown is made from small slabs of granite stuck to a board. A little sand is sprinkled on the board for greater realism.

MATERIALS:
- Pieces of bark
- Paints
- PVA glue
- Sharp knife

HOUSES

Draw a design on the surface of the bark with the point of the knife.

Then begin to carve the bark with the knife, as shown in the drawing.

Bark is built up in layers which separate fairly easily. Carve very carefully so that the design does not disintegrate.

Some of the windows on the houses shown have been left standing out and others carved inward, to give more variety.

Similarly, the front can be carved with one side standing out more than the other, to give added depth.

The roofs are flat pieces of bark glued on top of the houses.

The door and window frames are painted in to make them stand out more.

The woman is cut from a single piece of bark. The feet are added later, and fastened in place with drops of glue. Paint in the woman's hair, to give a better shape to the face.

MOTHER AND CHILD

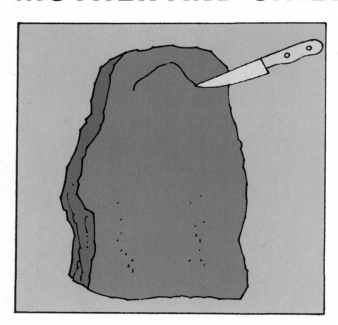

Draw the outline of the figure on the bark with the point of the knife.

Next, carve out the figure as shown in the drawing. Remember that the material can easily flake off in layers. You need to carve carefully and patiently.

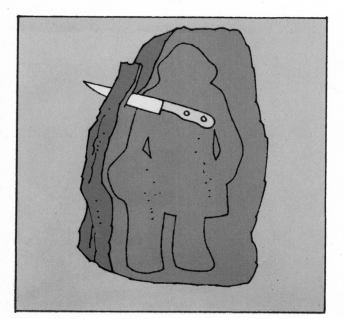

Make sure that the knife is very sharp, so that it cuts cleanly and does not leave a rough or crumbling edge.
The woman is carved from a single block. The bark should be thick enough for the feet to provide solid supports.

The child's feet should be carved separately and stuck onto the ends of the legs with drops of glue. The hair, the eyes and the spaces between the arms and the body should be picked out with paint to make the figures more realistic.

All kinds of simple figures can be carved in the same way, but remember that the material does not lend itself to very fine detail.

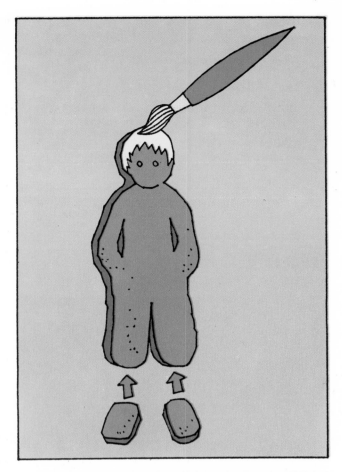

MATERIALS:
- Bark
- Stick
- Large leaves or paper
- PVA glue

BOAT

Draw the outline of the boat on a piece of bark.

Cut out the shape of the boat, then round it off to form the hull.
Make a hole in the middle of the deck to take the stick. The stick will be the mast.

The sails have been made from two pieces of corn leaf, but other sorts of leaf, or paper cut to size, will do. The sails are glued to the mast.

Finally, glue the mast into the hole in the hull.
Pine bark is a particularly good material for making boats of this kind. Since it is light in weight it floats very easily and can even carry small loads.

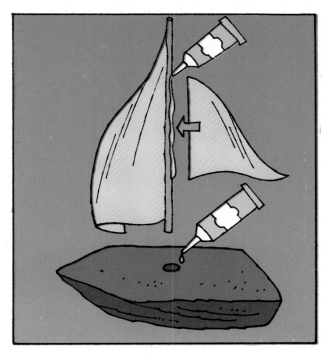

TRAY

Clean the pine cones thoroughly to remove all traces of dirt. Paint the cones and leave them to dry.

An oval board is useful for this project. Arrange the cones around the edge of the board, alternating the open cones with the closed ones. When you have decided on the position of each one, you can start glueing.

It is best to use a strong contact adhesive. Apply a drop to each cone and another to the board. Go right around the board, leaving the adhesive enough time to become tacky. Then press each cone down on the board and the adhesive will hold it firmly in position.

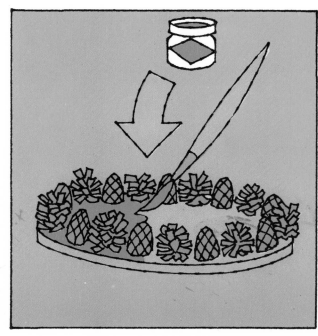

The tray can now be painted.

The finished tray makes an attractive
dish for nuts, sweets and dried fruit.

MATERIALS:
● Round cardboard box
● Small white shells
● Paint
● Small black beads
● PVA glue

SHELL BOX

Paint the cardboard box and wait until it is completely dry.

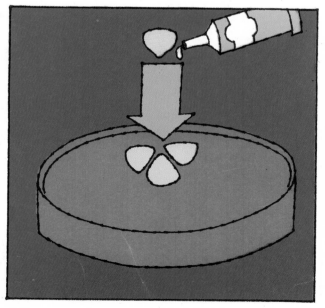

Decorate the inside edge of the lid with a line of small black beads, fixed on with a little glue. The black line contrasts well with the white of the shells.

A small black bead stuck in the center of each pattern will also help to set off the whiteness of the shells.

Arrange the shells in patterns and stick them down so as to cover the lid and bottom of the box. Make sure that the glue does not stain the cardboard around the shells; the best way of avoiding this is to apply a little glue to the shell itself before fixing it in position.

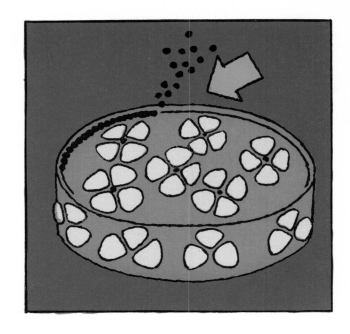

The finished box can be filled with sweets, marbles or sewing materials.

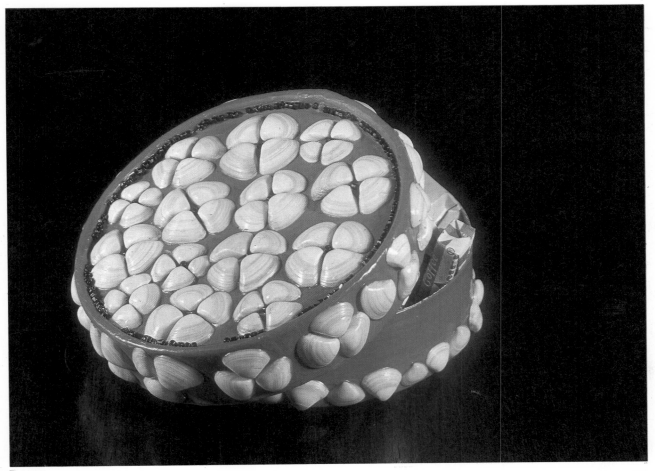

MATERIALS:
- Almonds
- Sunflower seeds
- Peanut
- Beads
- Grains of corn
- Hazelnut
- Walnut
- Shells
- PVA glue

TORTOISE, DUCK AND TOUCAN

TORTOISE

The body is made with an almond placed horizontally. The legs are four sunflower seeds. These should be stuck to the body and splayed out slightly to give an impression of movement and make a firm base.

The neck and head are made with a peanut. The eyes are two black beads stuck on either side of the head.

DUCK

An almond placed horizontally forms the body. This is supported on feet made of two grains of corn.
You will need to find two grains which are flat on one side, so that the body will stand evenly.

The head is a hazelnut, and the eyes are two red glass beads.

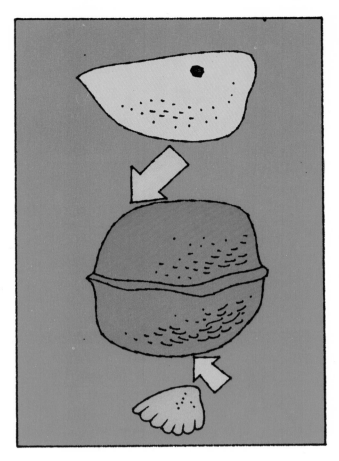

TOUCAN

The body is a walnut. The feet are formed by two small shells placed upside down. The head is made from an almond, with a black glass bead stuck on either side to form the eyes.

MATERIALS:
- Almond
- Melon seeds
- Peanut shells
- Two small glass beads
- PVA glue

OSTRICH

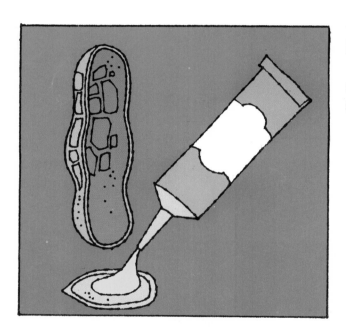

Choose two similar peanuts for the legs or cut a single shell neatly in half down the middle. Stick a large melon seed on the bottom of each shell for the feet.

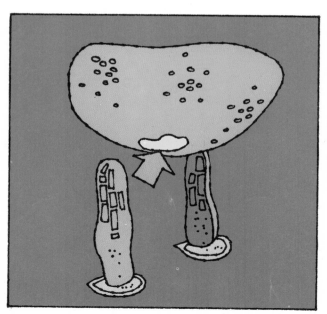

When the glue is dry, stick the legs to the underside of the almond. This forms the body. Make sure that the body stands firmly on its base.

The neck and head are made from a single peanut shell. The crest is made from half a melon seed and the other half of the same seed can be used for the beak. The two black beads for the eyes should be stuck on either side of the head.

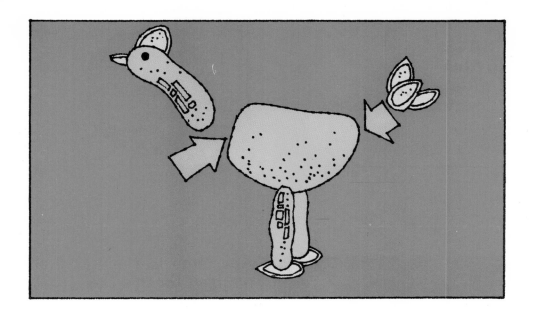

Finally, the neck is fastened to the main body of the bird.
The wings are each made from three melon seeds glued to the side of the body. It is best to stick the seeds on one by one and leave the glue on each seed to dry before attaching the next. The tail is made from two or more melon seeds glued to the rear. Stick on as many as are needed to balance the ostrich, so that the weight of the tail counteracts that of the head.

FAN

Any large leaf, suitably shaped, can be used for this fan.

The leaf should first be washed thoroughly to remove dirt, then pressed under some books for a number of days.

Next, paint the leaf on both sides with glue. This will give it a gloss and also make it strong and pliable.

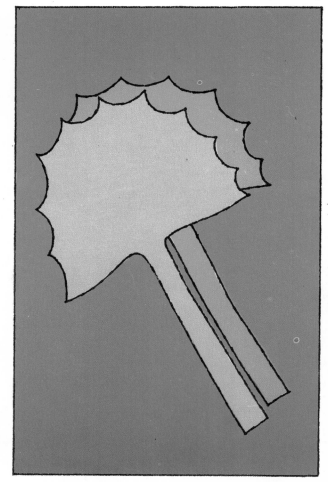

Cut two pieces of leather to the shape shown in the drawing and stick them on either side of the leaf.

Bind a thin strip of leather around the stem to reinforce it, as shown in the drawing. You can decorate the leather with a painted pattern.

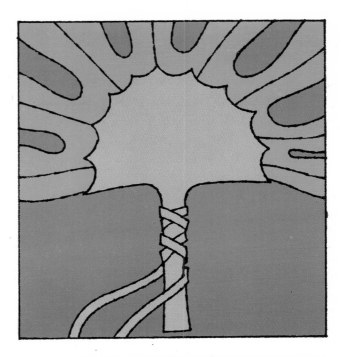

MOUSE

Choose a large shell for the base and fill it with plaster of Paris to give it weight. Make a narrow groove across the back of the shell.

Stick the two mussel shells together, and then glue them into the groove in the base shell, so that they are standing on end.

Stick on the small shells for the buttons, the ears and the mouse's hat.

Paint the shells in different colors and paint the eyes at the top of the body. Stick some strands of thread beneath the eyes to form the whiskers. Use very little glue and make sure that it does not spread to the paint, or the face will be spoiled.

This comical mouse is just one example of how you can use shells to make simple but attractive decorations.

BIRDS, CATS AND ALLIGATOR

When you have collected the pebbles, try and see how they can be made to suggest animals. This project shows examples of how some animals can be made.

The large bird is made from two pebbles; one forms the body, the other the head and beak. The eyes, the beak and the mottling on the body and head are painted in. The head is fixed to the body with a drop of glue. The ducks are each made from two stones stuck together. A red stripe marks the beak and the eyes are two dots of color.

The kittens are made of two pebbles—the head and the body. The larger cat also has an upraised tail. The different pieces are glued together and supported with books while they dry. The eyes are painted onto the head; the pupils are simply spots of green or black. The whites of the eyes are either painted in or else formed by a white vein in the stone itself.

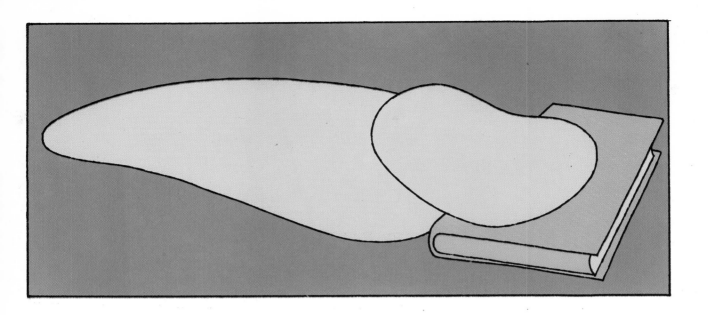

The alligator has more of its features painted in and the two stones from which it is made are more carefully chosen for their shape.
The two pieces are glued together, and the head is supported with a book while it dries. The eyes, nostrils and a grinning row of teeth are painted in on the head. The body is painted in a crisscross pattern to represent the alligator's scales.

COUNTRY SCENE

Arrange the shells on the card to make up the picture you have in mind. Once the final design of the picture is decided upon, the shells can be stuck down on the card.

A small amount of glue around the edge of each shell will be enough to fix it in position. Make sure that the glue does not stain the card around the shells, or it will produce dark shadows which will spoil the scene.

Once the picture is completed and the glue is dry, the card can be mounted in a frame or simply fastened to the wall with drawing pins.

MATERIALS:
- Six large snail shells
- Paints or felt pens
- A piece of square card
- Strips of white card or adhesive tape
- PVA glue

THREE IN A ROW

Paint the snails in two different colors—three red and three green for example.

Stick the white strips onto the square to make the 'tracks' which the snails must follow during the game.

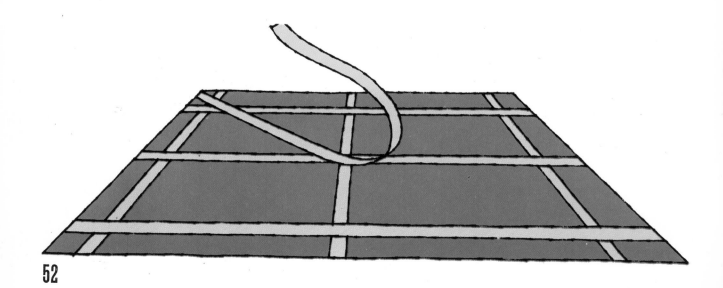

When the snails are dry, you can start to play. The two players each have three pieces. They take it in turn to place their pieces on the intersections of the white lines. Still playing in turn, they can then move their pieces from one intersection to another. The first one who manages to get his three pieces in a straight line is the winner.

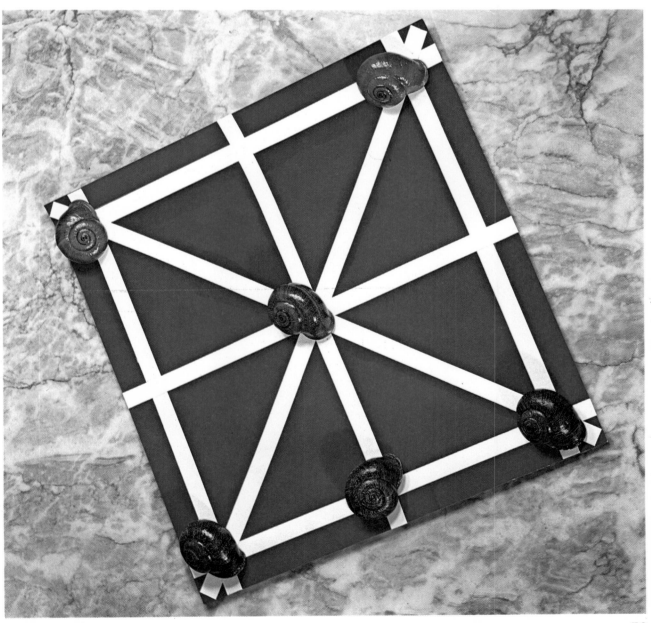

CATERPILLAR

On a walk in a park or in the country you can often find a piece of wood, or a stone or root, which suggests a particular object or animal.

The piece of root shown here, for example, was found lying on the ground and looked exactly like a caterpillar.

It was taken home and washed thoroughly to remove the dirt, then left to dry. Before starting to color it we looked at a book about insects and found that the root was shaped very like the caterpillar of the Polyphemus moth; so we decided to paint the root in the appropriate colors.

The best results are often achieved with the simplest decoration.

BRACELET

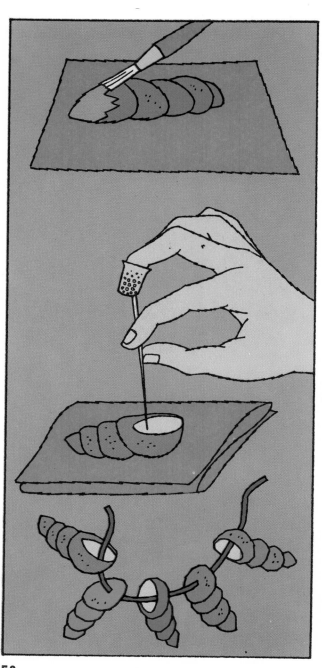

Wash the shells, both inside and out, to remove any dirt. When they are dry, paint them in different colors.

Once the paint is dry, the shells can be pierced to take the elastic. This is best done on a padded surface such as a piece of cloth folded in four, or a piece of foam rubber. Press gently on the needle and it will go through the shell.

Now thread the shells onto the thin elastic, alternating the colors. The elastic should then be tied tightly into a loop.

The same method can be used to make a necklace, but then it is better to use a length of nylon thread rather than elastic. The thread will allow the shells to hang freely, whereas the elastic holds them tightly around the wrist of the wearer.

MATERIALS:
- Snail shells in different sizes
- A chain with a clasp
- A piece of nylon thread
- A stout needle and thimble
- Paints

NECKLACE

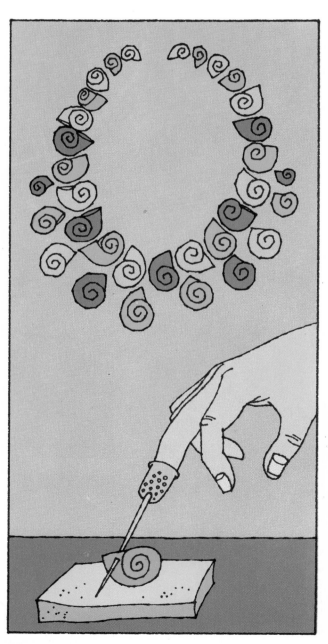

First wash the shells in warm water and leave them to dry.

Arrange the shells in the pattern required for the necklace, and then paint them.

Once the paint is dry, pierce holes in the shells to take the nylon thread, using a stout needle and a suitably padded surface.

Thread the shells onto the nylon thread and attach them to the chain as shown in the drawing.

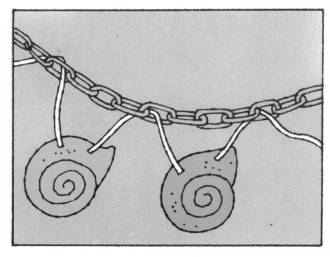

A second row of shells can be added to enlarge the necklace, as shown in the drawing.

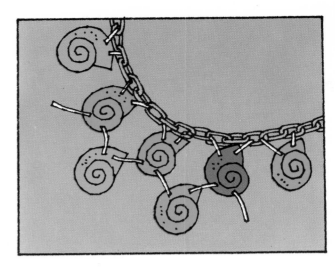

With the three basic elements—shells, thread and chain—you can produce necklaces in a variety of different patterns. This is just one example of what can be done.

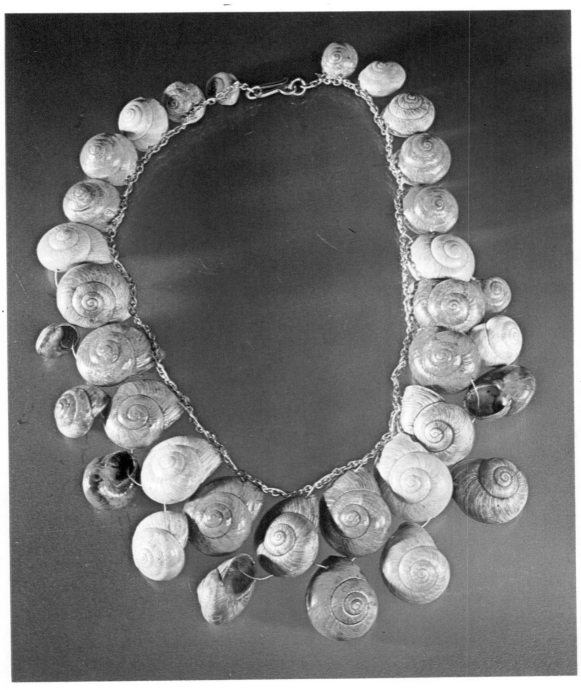

HEADS

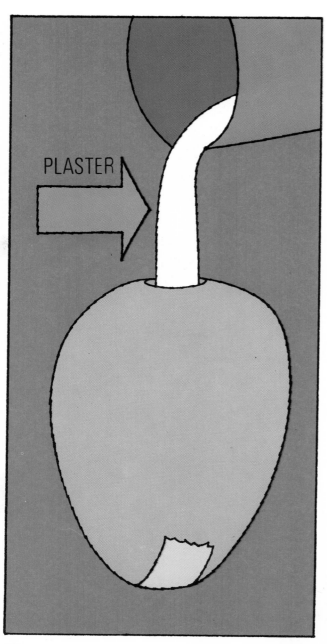

Empty the egg shells by piercing a small hole in each end and blowing through one of them.

Once the shells are empty and clean, fill them with plaster of Paris. To do this, cover one of the holes with a piece of adhesive tape and pour in the plaster of Paris through the other hole. Wipe off any plaster which gets onto the outside of the shell.

When the plaster of Paris has hardened, glue each shell to a piece of cardboard. As soon as the glue is dry, you can paint the eggs however you wish. The feather shown in the photograph is glued to the top of the egg.

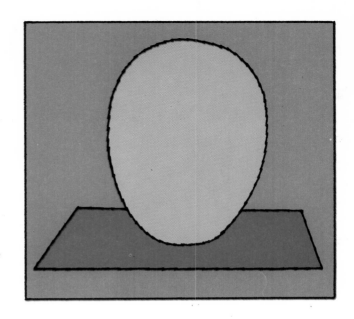

These figures can be used as place cards for a party. The names of the guests can be written on the cardboard base.

FLOWER AND VASE

Place the flowers between two sheets of blotting paper and leave them pressed under some books for a few days until they are dry.

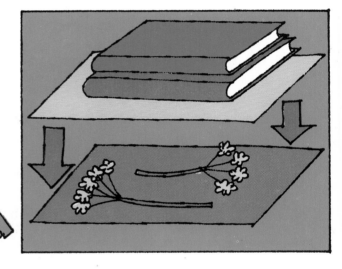

Trace the outline of the vase on the yellow felt with glue.

Pour sand over the glue and press it lightly with the fingers, so that it sticks firmly in place.

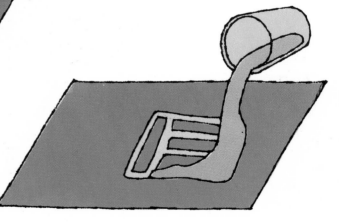

When the glue has dried, blow away the excess sand. Arrange the flowers on the felt in an attractive bouquet.

Stick each flower in position with a few drops of glue. Apply the glue carefully so as not to stain the felt.

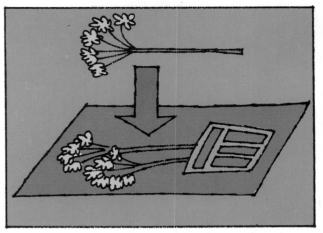

ORNAMENTAL EGGS

Empty the eggs by piercing a hole in each end and blowing out the contents. Wash the shells thoroughly and leave them to dry. If they are even slightly damp, the colors will tend to run and spoil the effect of the decoration.

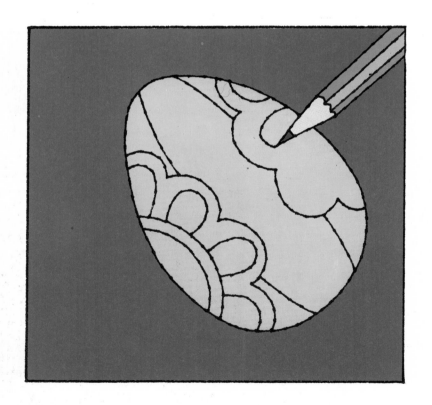

When decorating an egg, sketch in the design with a pencil before applying the colors. Decorating a curved surface is not as easy as it may appear.

When you are satisfied with your design, color it in with the felt pens. The felt pens will cover the pencil marks.

When you have finished color-
ing the eggs, apply a coat of
varnish.

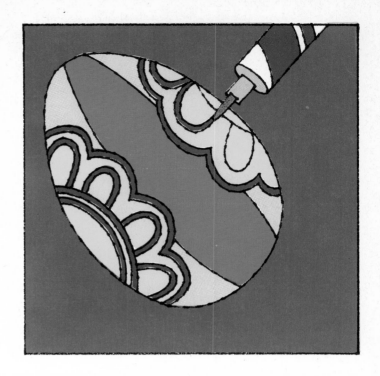

PENCIL AND PEN HOLDERS

As a pencil is used up it gets so short that it becomes difficult to hold. This is when a pencil holder comes in useful.

To make a pencil holder, take a thickish piece of cane and make three slots at one end as shown in the drawing.

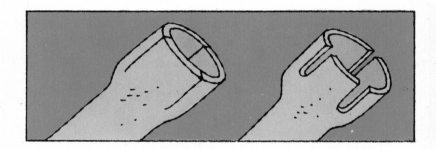

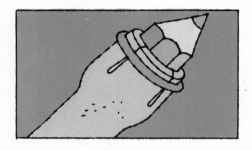

Paint the holder and, when the paint has dried, insert the pencil in the slotted end. Fix the rubber band around the three segments so that the cane closes tightly around the pencil.

The pen holder is made with a narrower piece of cane. Make a cut in one end and insert the shank of the pen nib into this cut.
A ring of wider cane clamps the nib in position, as shown in the drawing.

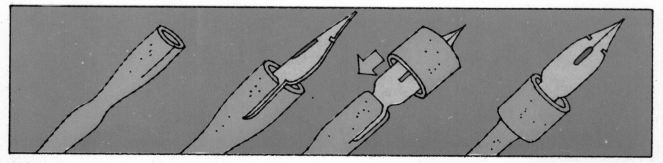

If the inside of the ring is too small, it should be hollowed out until it fits tightly onto the narrower piece of cane. If it is too wide, the inside should be filled out with gummed paper until it is the right size.

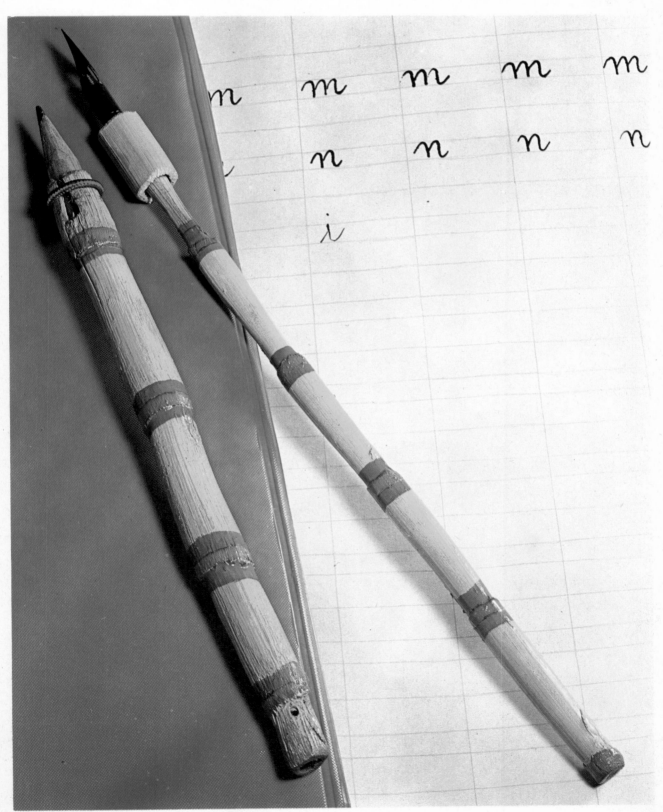

MATERIALS:
● **Walnut shell halves**
● **Pieces of leather**
● **PVA glue**
● **A brace and bit**

BUTTONS

Drill two holes in each half shell. The holes should be cleanly drilled, without any cracks or splinters around the edge. Rough holes will wear through the strips of leather which are to be threaded through them.

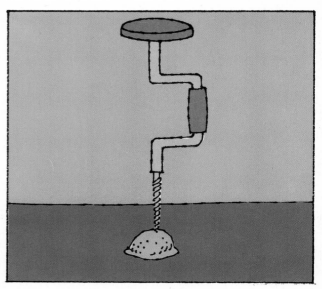

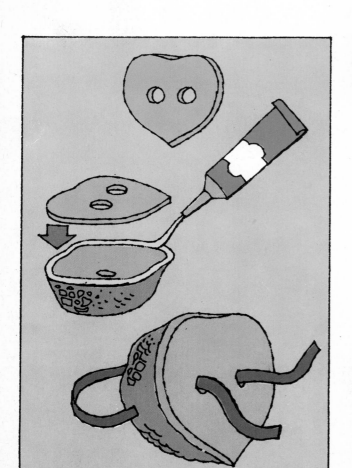

Cut several pieces of leather the same shape as the base of the shells. Make two holes in each piece of leather corresponding to the holes in the shells.

Glue each piece of leather to the base of a shell.

Pass a thin strip of leather through the holes in the shell and the leather backing.

Thread the strips of leather onto a stout darning needle and pass them through the cloth of the garment. Finally, tie the two ends of the strip in a knot so that the button is firmly fixed.

If the garment does not have any button holes, take another strip of leather and thread it through the material, knotting it into a loop as shown in the drawing.

STONE MEN

Find stones to make up the different parts of each figure—legs, bodies, heads, and in some cases arms. The pebbles which serve as buttons on some of the figures are not essential, but they help to give the figures more character.

The flat stones which form the base of each figure are, however, important, since without them it would be very difficult to make the figures stand upright.

Start by glueing the legs to the flat base, then mount the body on top of the legs, waiting for the glue to dry at each stage.

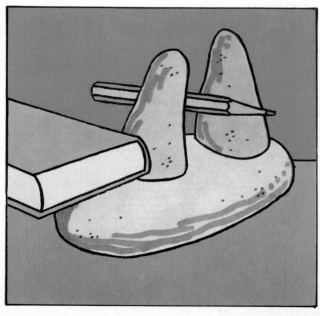

When each figure is finished it can be varnished to bring out the colors. When the varnish has dried, you can paint in the details.

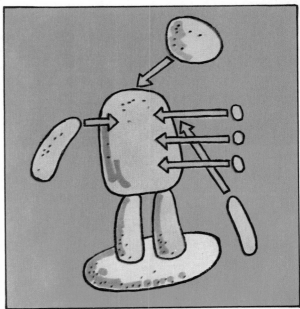

The head is then glued on top of the body, followed by the arms. Support the head, with a box or some books for example, while the glue is drying.

BROOM

MATERIALS:
- A bamboo cane
- Thin twigs
- String
- Paints
- PVA glue

Smooth off any roughness at the knots in the cane, especially where your hand will grip it. This will prevent splinters getting in your hand when you use the broom. Collect the twigs into small bunches and bind these tightly at one end with string.

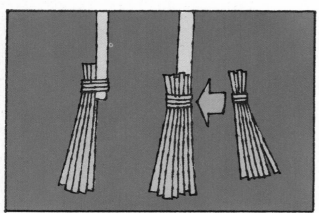

Next, arrange the bunches around the end of the broom handle, tying each one separately in place. All the bunches should then be bound together tightly, as shown in the drawing, and the binding reinforced with plenty of glue.

When the glue is dry, the broom handle can be painted in different colors.

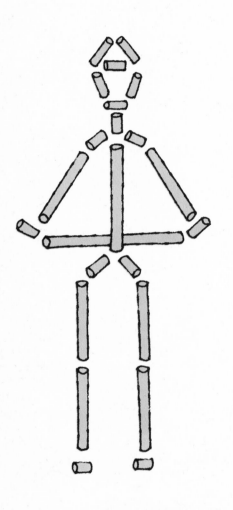

ACROBAT

Cut pieces of cane to make up the outline of the figure, as shown in the drawing.

Cut pieces of wire about 1 in. longer than the pieces of cane. Pass a length of wire through each cane and bend the ends into a hook with a pair of pliers. The different parts of the figure are then hooked together and the hooks closed up with the pliers. The hands and feet are made as shown in the drawing below.

When the figure is completed, attach a long piece of wire to the top of the head. Make an open hook at the top end of the wire, so that the figure can be hung up.

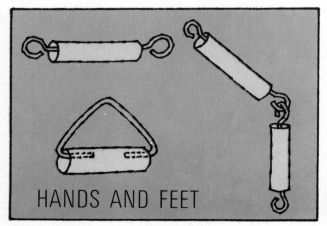

HANDS AND FEET

The figure should hang straight. If it hangs crookedly, this means that one side is heavier than the other. It should be possible to avoid this by making the sections on each side exactly the same length. However, if the figure does come out un-balanced, trim one of the sections on the heavier side.

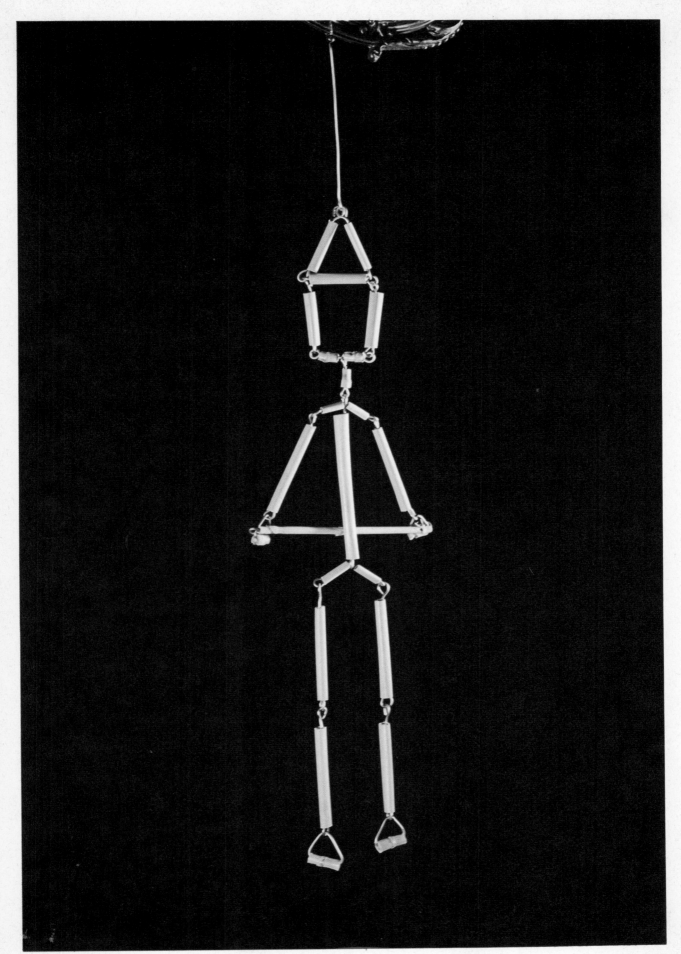

STONE AGE WEAPONS

Working stone requires skill and physical strength, and can only be done successfully after a lot of practice. It is quite easy, however, to find stones which are already shaped like the axe, spear and arrowheads made by prehistoric men.

Arrow- and spearheads are bound to pieces of cane as shown below. The leather thong must be bound very tightly so as to keep the stone firmly in place. Moisten the thong before using it, so that the binding will shrink tight as the leather dries.

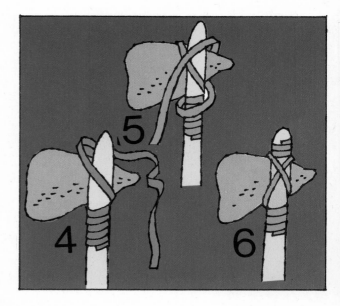

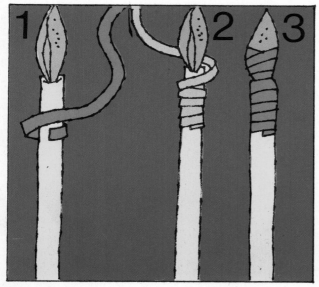

Flat pieces of rock with sharp or notched edges are useful, and can be bound to a handle with a leather thong, as shown above, to make a stone axe.

76

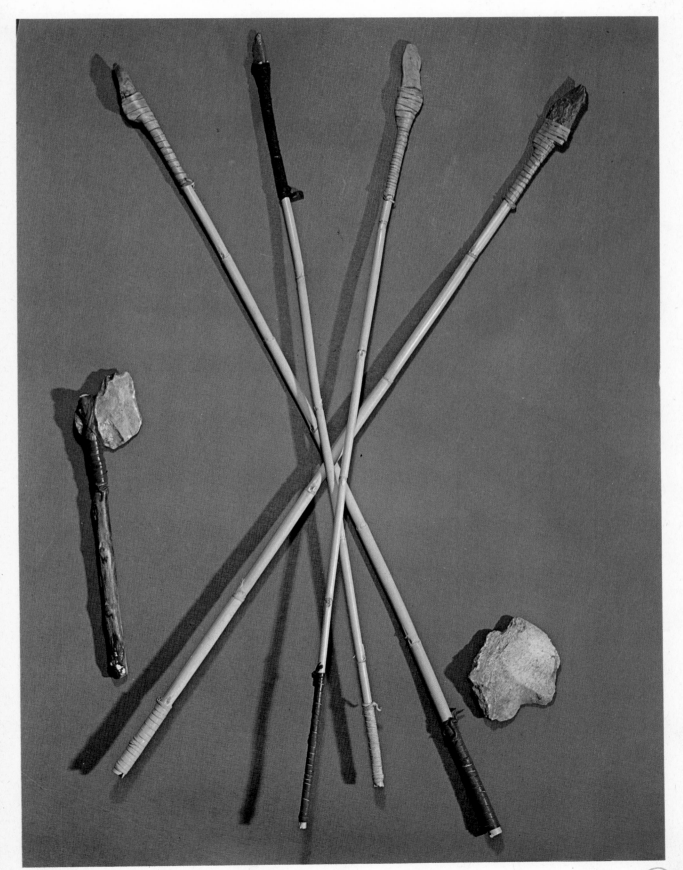

MATERIALS:
- Sticks
- Large leaves
- Raffia or string for the hair
- Poster paints
- Two flat pieces of soft wood
- Two pins and PVA glue

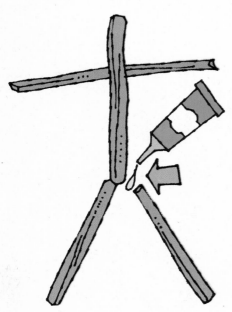

SCARECROW

Make the skeleton of the scarecrow from sticks, joining them with plenty of glue.

Stick strands of raffia or string to the head to make the hair.

The hat is made from a leaf bent into a cup shape, as shown in the drawing, and glued on top of the hair.

The jacket and trousers are leaves colored brightly with poster paints, then wrapped around the figure and glued in place.
Shred the sleeves with a pair of scissors after they have been stuck onto the arms.

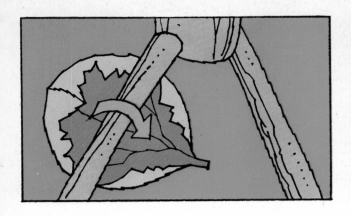
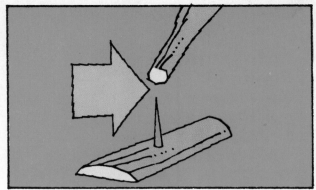

The two pieces of soft wood form the feet and should be large, so that the scarecrow will stand upright.

Push a pin through each of the feet, as shown, and into the ends of the legs.

MATERIALS:
- Bark
- Fresh autumn leaves
- PVA glue
- Colored card
- Waxed paper

TREE

Autumn leaves have a whole range of vivid colors, running from golden brown to red. Prepare the leaves so that they retain some flexibility and do not crumble or break. To do this, place each leaf between two sheets of waxed paper, and pass a warm iron over the top. The wax in the paper will melt and impregnate the leaf, giving it a glossy sheen which will last for a long time.

The trunk of the tree is made from pieces of thin, soft bark.

When all the pieces have been prepared, lay the tree out on the piece of card. Once the final design has been decided upon, the pieces can be glued in position. Do not use too much glue or you will spoil the design.

The finished picture can be framed in dark wood, which will bring out the colors of the leaves, or can be fastened directly to the wall with drawing pins.

81

LEAF COLLAGE

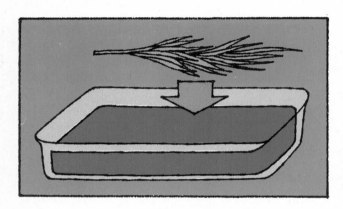

An infinite variety of arrangements can be made with dried grasses, leaves, flowers and even small fruits. The different parts of the collage can be used in their natural colors, or all or some of them can be dyed.

To dye leaves or grasses, mix some dye with water, and soak the leaves thoroughly. Then hang them up to dry and spread out some sheets of newspaper to catch the drips.

Once all the parts of the design have been prepared they can be arranged on the card. Then, when the final arrangement has been decided upon, stick them down.
Do not use too much glue or it will stain the card and make an ugly outline around the edges of the leaves. When the glue is dry, the collage can be framed and hung up on the wall.

WALKING STICKS

Straight sticks are quite easy to find, and you can also be lucky enough to find a straight stick with a joint or curve at one end, which forms a ready made handle.

Clean the stick, and give it several coats of varnish.

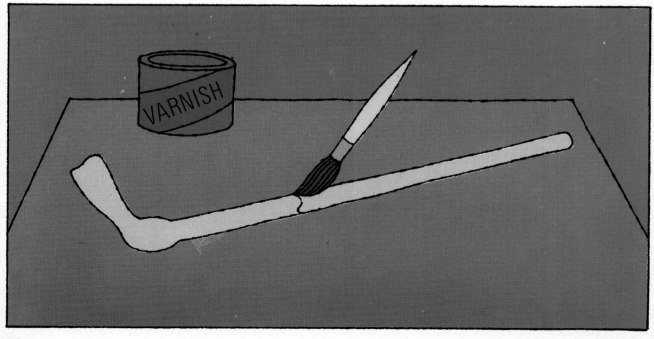

VARNISH

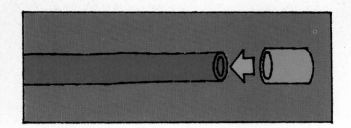

Fit a rubber tip at the bottom end of the stick. This deadens the blow as the cane strikes the ground and prevents it from splitting; it also prevents the tip from skidding.

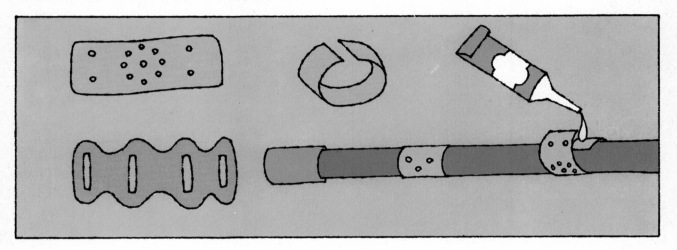

Decorate the stick with leather bands glued at regular intervals, as shown in the drawing. The bands also serve as reinforcements.
The handle of the walking stick can be covered in leather to make it more comfortable. The shape of the covering will naturally vary according to the shape of the stick used.

A long staff can be decorated with braided wool cords. The cords are attached to the end of the staff by a leather strip, as shown in the drawing.

(The woolen cords and pompoms are made as described in volume 6 of Color Crafts, page 78.)

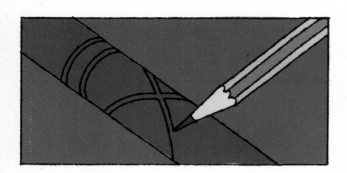

To make a carved stick, it is best to choose a stick which is still slightly green; you will then be able to make finer cuts and the wood is less likely to split. Start by drawing on the design in pencil. Make parallel lines where the bark is to be cut away.

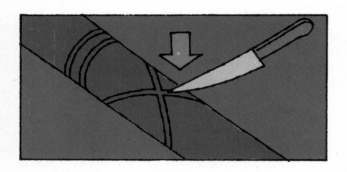

When the design is complete, you can start work with the knife. Remember to keep it at right angles to the bark, and keep the hand which is not cutting out of harm's way.

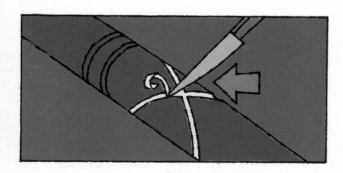

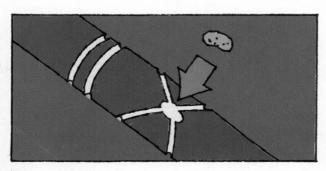

The stick can also be decorated with small stones or shells. Make a small hollow to fit each one; if the ornament is glued directly onto the bark it will soon rub off.
Put some glue in the hollow and press the pebble or shell into it, maintaining the pressure until the glue is completely dry.

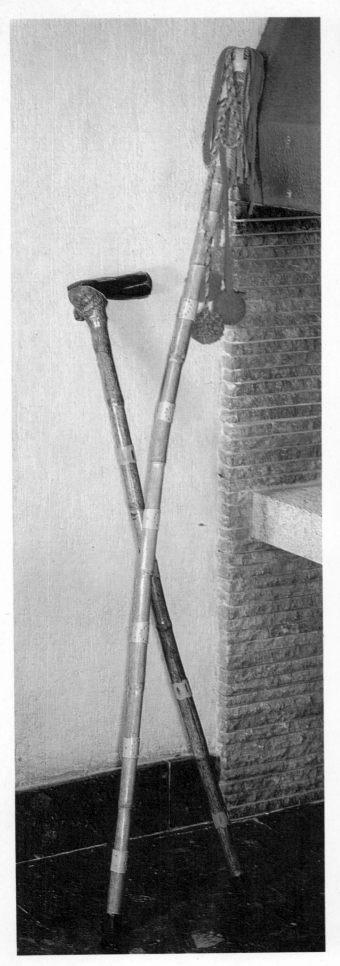

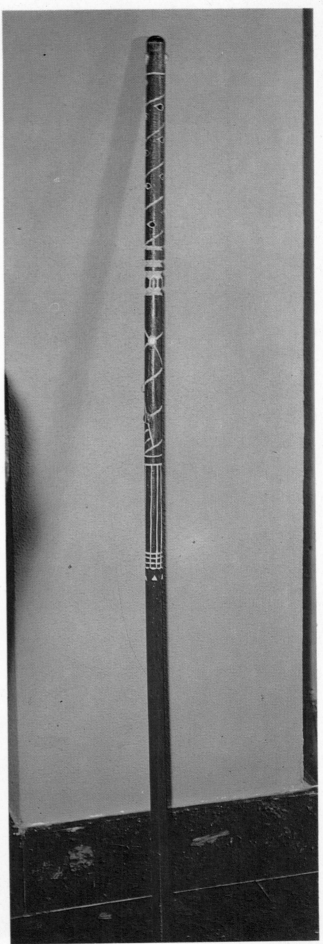

MATERIALS:
- A large open pine cone
- Two twigs or long cones
- An orange
- Three small plum pits
- Feathers

WITCH DOCTOR

The large pine cone must stand evenly on its base. It may be necessary to cut off the bottom layer of the cone or sandpaper it flat.

Impale the orange on top of the cone.

Stick the three plum pits into the orange to form the face—two for the eyes and one for the mouth. The feathers are then stuck into the top of the orange to form the headdress.

The arms are made from two twigs or elongated cones which are simply wedged between the scales of the large pine cone.

You can paint the arms and body, or
leave them in plain wood.

MATERIALS:
- Flat stones
- Small rounded pebbles
- PVA glue
- Leather cord
- A masonry drill mounted in a brace
- Clear varnish
- Wire and pliers

MEDALLIONS

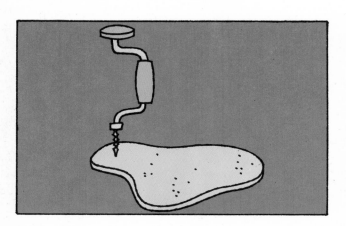

Using the masonry drill, make a hole near the edge of each flat stone.

Choose a number of rounded pebbles and make a design on top of the flat stone. When you have decided what the design is to be, fix each pebble to the stone with a drop of glue.

As soon as the glue is dry, give the whole medallion a coat of varnish.

Make a ring of wire and pass it through the hole in the medallion. Close the ring up with the help of the pliers, if necessary.

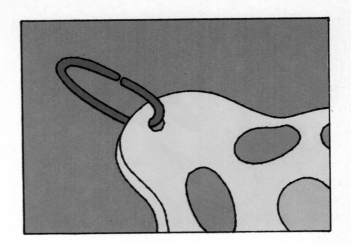

Finally, pass the leather cord through the ring and tie it into a loop.

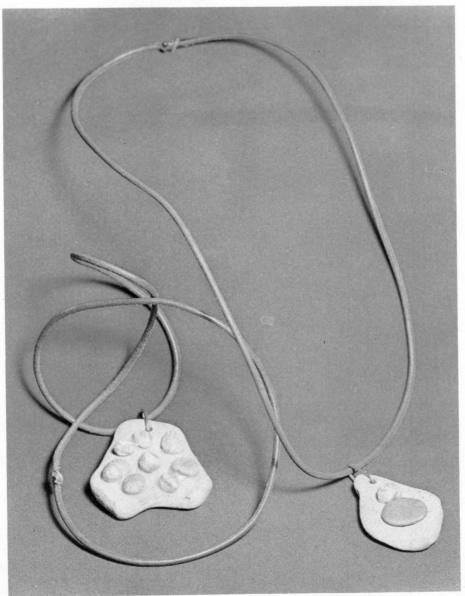

MATERIALS:
- Pieces of cane
- String
- Some strands of raffia or thread
- Straws
- PVA glue

RAFT

The lengths of cane are tied together as shown in the drawing. It is best to moisten the string before you start. String stretches a little when moist and then shrinks again when dry. If the string is dry when you use it, the joints will loosen when the raft is placed in the water.
Tie the ends tightly to make sure that they do not come undone.

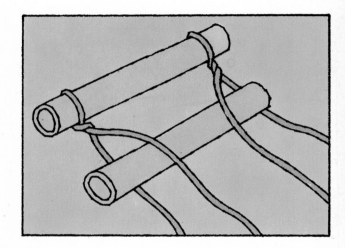

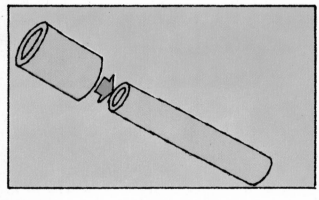

The body of the fisherman is made from a piece of cane.
The head is a slightly thicker piece of cane, which fits on top of the body. A few strands of raffia or thread are stuck on top of the head to make the hair.

The arms are two thick straws which are stuck to the body and bent at the joints.
The legs are two thick straws which are fitted into the bottom of the body. They are also bent, to make the thighs, shins and feet.

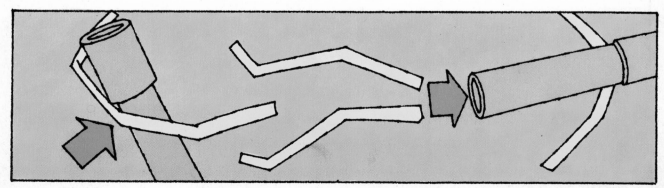

Cut a slot at the lower end of the body, at the back, so that the figure can be bent into a sitting position. Now paint the figure, using different colors for the shirt and trousers if you like.

The fisherman is seated on the raft and supported by a short length of cane, like a barrel, which is glued in position.
Tie the fisherman to the raft with a piece of string around his waist to prevent him from falling into the water.

The fishing rod is a thick straw with a piece of thread tied to one end. Attach a cork to the end of the line as a float.

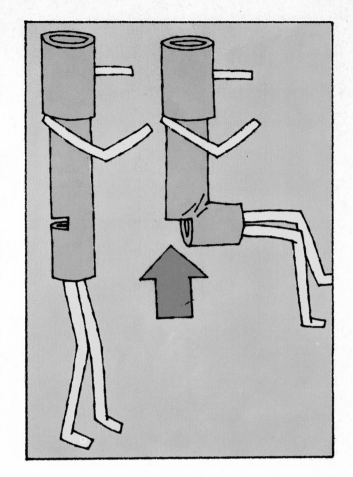

FLUTE AND WHISTLE

To make a flute, choose a piece of bamboo with a knot at one end and a second knot in the middle. The inside of the middle knot will have to be broken through so that the air can circulate freely inside the tube.

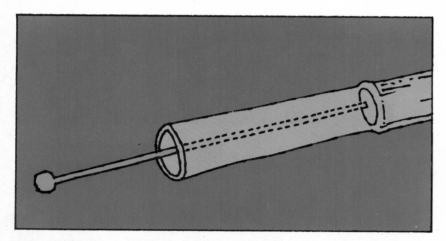

The end knot should be left closed for the flute to sound properly. Start by making a hole 5 in. from the closed end, and a smaller one 3 in. from the first. Now you can try the flute for sound.

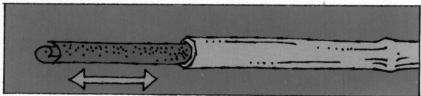

Smooth out the inside of the flute by rolling up a piece of sandpaper and working it up and down through the open end.

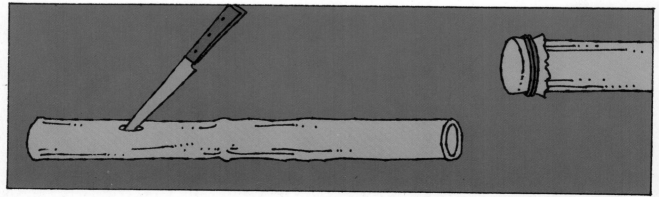

In some cases you will find that the flute sounds better if the open end is covered with a piece of paper, held on with a rubber band.

Blow across the hole nearest the end of the flute, placing your mouth as shown in the drawing.

Once you have tried the sound produced with the first finger hole, you can work out the intervals at which the others should be made to produce the different notes—nearer to the first hole for the higher notes and farther away for the lower ones.

To make a whistle, rub an apricot pit on a piece of sandpaper until a hole appears.

You can make a hole in one end and extract the kernel, then place the stone against your bottom lip and blow across the hole.

Alternatively, you can make a hole in each side and extract the kernel, then place the stone in front of your teeth and close your lips around it. Now blow hard and the air passing through the two holes will produce a piercing whistle.

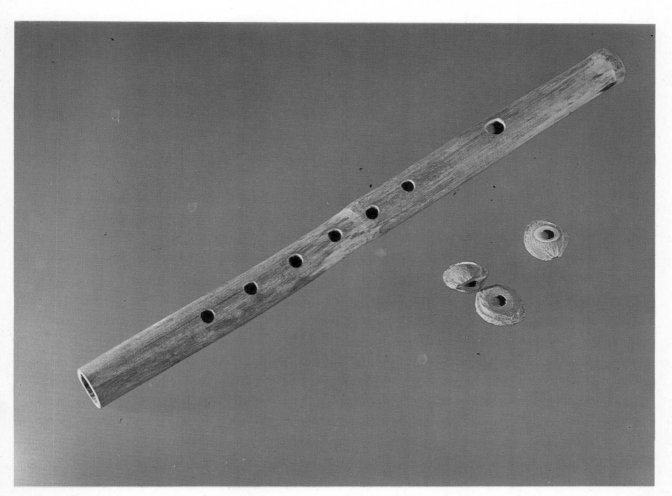

GUINEA PIG

Take a stone and try to see what animal it can suggest. Then add extra pieces to complete the animal. This is the way in which this guinea pig was made.

First we found a reddish stone which looked like a head, and even had a clearly marked eye-hole. Then we looked for a larger stone which could form the body for this head.

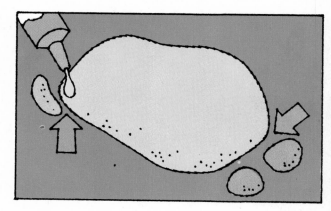

The rest of the stones were easier to find—two similar ones for the ears, two small pebbles for the forepaws and a long stone for the tail.

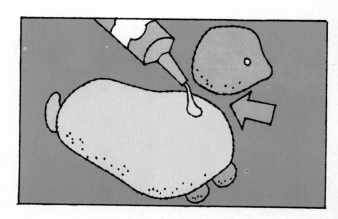

All the stones were given a coat of clear varnish to give them a gloss and bring out the colors. When the varnish was completely dry, the stones were stuck in position with drops of glue, and supported with books while they dried.

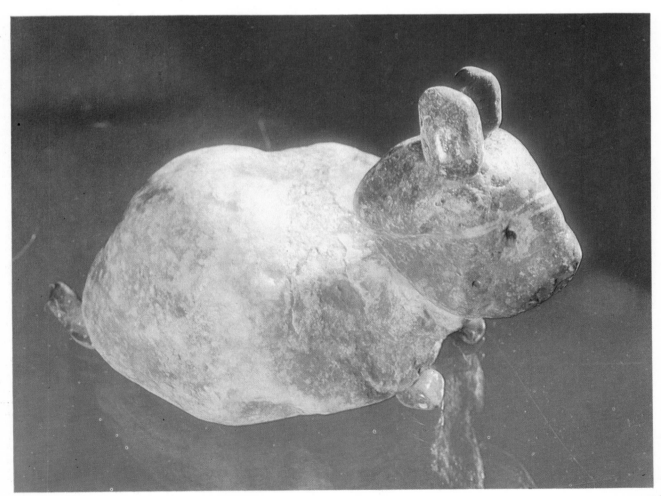

NECK BAND

Some Indian tribes of North America wear ornaments made of feathers for their ceremonial dances. These can be worn on the legs or arms, or around the neck. The ornaments can be made to suggest birds or flowers.

To make this neck band, cut the leather to the shape shown in the drawing. If the leather tends to curl up, cut two pieces and stick them together.

Draw the outline of the design on the leather and then stick the feathers in position. Since feathers are very light, only a little glue will be needed to keep them in place.
The glue should be applied to the central shaft of the feather; be careful not to get any on the barbs or these will become stiff instead of soft and pliable.

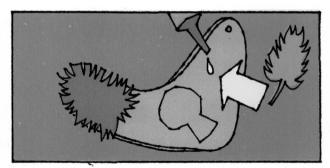

When the design is finished, cut a strip of leather and pass it through the holes at either end of the leather backing. The ends of the strip are stuck on the back with glue.

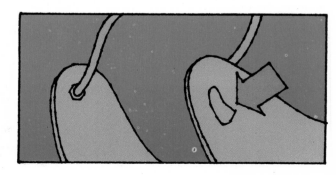

CLOWN

Glue the shells for the legs one on top of the other. Make each leg separately When the glue is dry, place the legs in position and add the shells for the body on top.

Use the glue sparingly. If too much is used, the shells will tend to slide out of position. Reinforce the joints with more glue once the first coat is dry, if necessary.

The arms are made separately from the body, and the shells can be arranged so that the arms appear slightly curved.

The shells used for the hands should be of a different color from the arms so that they stand out. Glue the arms in position.

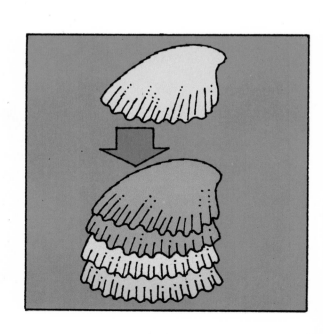

You can add extra color to the figure by sticking colored string around the edge of each shell, but this is not essential.

The head is composed of two large shells glued together as shown in the drawing, with the hair sandwiched between them. When the glue is dry, the hair can be combed back and tied in a pigtail with a piece of colored string.

Draw in the face with felt pens.

Make a slot in the top of the body to take the head and glue the head in position. When the glue is dry, stick another shell on top of the head to make a hat.

The join between the head and the body can be reinforced with colored string soaked in glue, which will also give the clown a brightly colored collar.

TOTEM

Stick together three of the large shells as shown in the drawing.

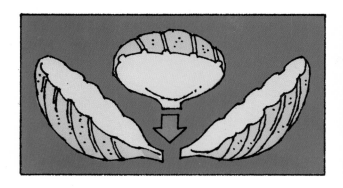

These are then stuck vertically on top of the fourth large shell to form a solid base for the figure. Two small shells can reinforce the base. Make sure that these 'feet' lie flat.

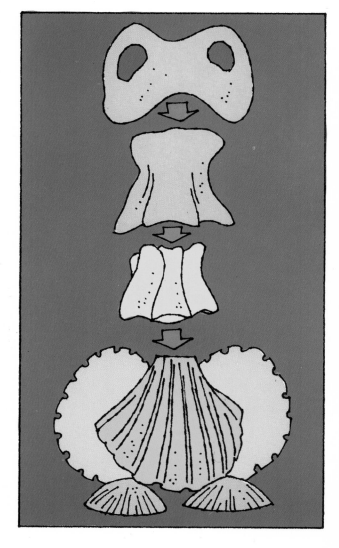

When the base is firm and stable, the bones can be arranged on top of it. The three bones shown here are from an oxtail, but any other type can be used as long as they are a suitable shape and size.
When the glue holding the bones has dried, the totem can be painted.

MATERIALS:
- Pieces of cane of different thicknesses
- Sharp knife
- PVA glue
- A piece of thick, soft wire

GRASSHOPPER

Use the thickest piece of cane to make the outside of the grasshopper's body.

The knotted end of this piece can be rounded off to make the grasshopper's face.

Cut a rectangle from the grasshopper's back and then shape the sides to make wing covers, as shown in the first drawing.
Cut another piece of cane about the same length as the body and small enough to slide inside it.
Cut this piece as shown in the second drawing to make the tail end of the grasshopper.
Slide it into the body and fix it in place with a couple of drops of glue.

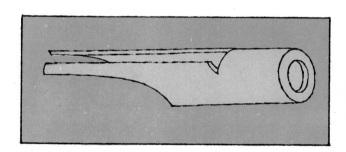

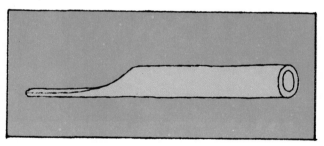

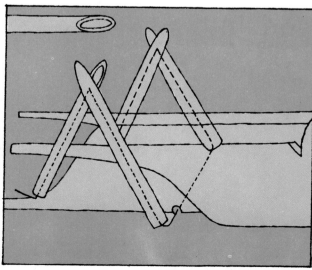

The back legs are each made from two pieces of cane, bevelled off at the joins so that the angle of the legs can be changed. Make a hole in either side of the body, about half way along. Pass the wire through the holes and through both leg pieces, bending the wire over at the end to form the feet.

Make four small holes in the head and insert two short pieces of cane for the eyes and two long ones to form the antennae.
Make two holes under the body and insert two pieces of cane to make the front legs.

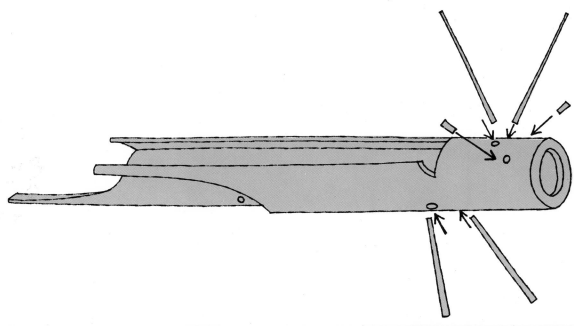

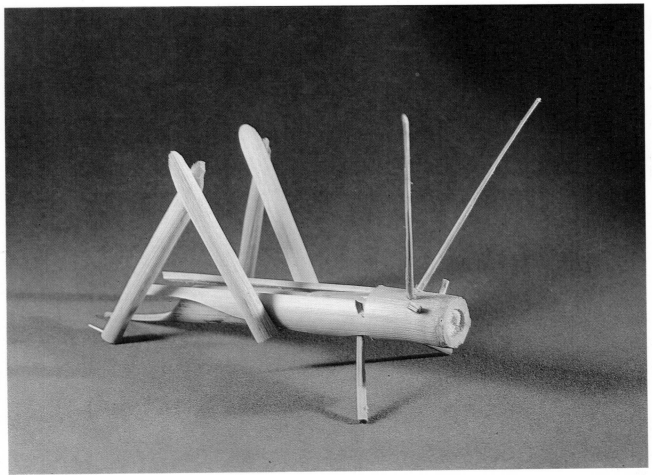

ARTICULATED DOLL

Cut lengths of cane or straw for the different parts of the body—head, trunk, arms, legs and feet.

Take a long piece of wire and bend it in half. Pass the double wire through the trunk and the head, then thread the pieces for the legs and feet onto the two ends.

The arms are threaded onto a separate piece of wire, which is bent around the neck as shown in the drawing. Make a hook at each end to keep the pieces from coming off.

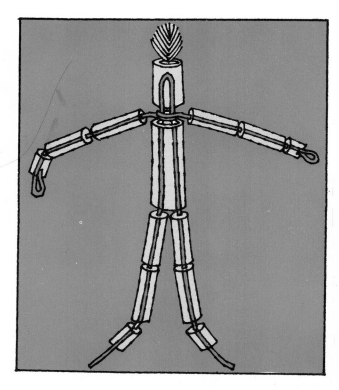

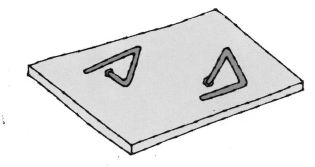

The ear of corn is fitted into the top of the head to form the hair, and the raffia is wound around the neck like a scarf.

Make two holes in the base and pass through them the two ends of wire protruding from the feet. Bend the ends under the board as shown. Now the doll can be painted.

The wire skeleton enables the doll to be bent into different positions, while the solid base prevents it from falling over.

MATERIALS:
- **Sticks of different thicknesses and lengths**
- **Raffia or wood wool**
- **Leaves**
- **A slab of cork or polystyrene**
- **PVA glue**
- **A piece of green crêpe paper**
- **Hair spray**

A SHEPHERD AND HIS FLOCK

Cover the cork base with the green crêpe paper.

Make the skeleton of the shepherd with sticks of different sizes. Stick the raffia or wood wool to the head to form the hair and beard as shown in the drawing. Spray them with hair spray so that they keep their shape.

The skeletons of the sheep are each made with five sticks glued together as shown in the drawing.
Raffia or wood wool is then glued to the body and fixed with hair spray. Any ends which stick out and spoil the shape of the body can be cut off with sharp scissors.

The shepherd's hand is fixed to the top of his stick with a drop of glue. His clothes are made from leaves which are glued to the body and can be painted with poster paints to make them more colorful.

Fix small leaves to the branches of
the tree with drops of glue.

The shepherd, tree and sheep are fixed in holes made in the cork base.

109

MATERIALS:
- Pieces of straw
- PVA glue
- An ear of corn

BUTTERFLY

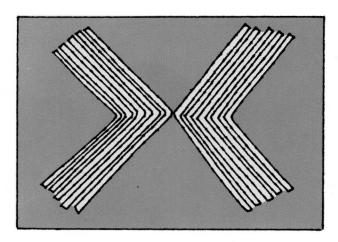

Cut the straw into pieces of roughly the same length. Bend them in the middle as shown, taking care not to break them. Now arrange the bent straws to make the two wings as shown in the drawing.

Add four more bent straws above and below to complete the wings.

Now arrange three bent straws on each wing as shown below and fix them in position with plenty of glue, so that they hold all the straws together.

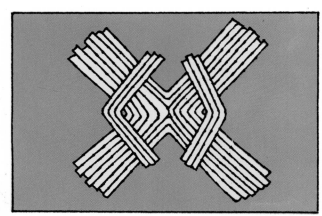

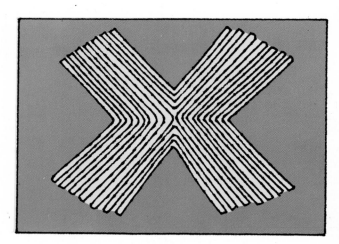

Two more straws are glued to the underside to reinforce the butterfly.

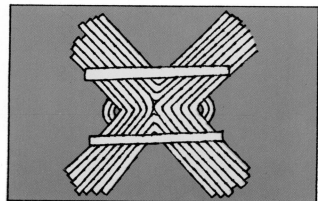

The butterfly's body is made from an ear of corn with the grains removed. Glue a small piece of straw to the end of the ear and insert into this two strands from the tip of the ear, again glueing them in position. These strands often have tiny bulbs on the end and make realistic antennae.

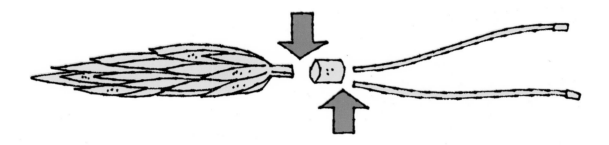

When the butterfly is completed and the glue has dried thoroughly, trim off the wings with a sharp pair of scissors, so that they are symmetrical.

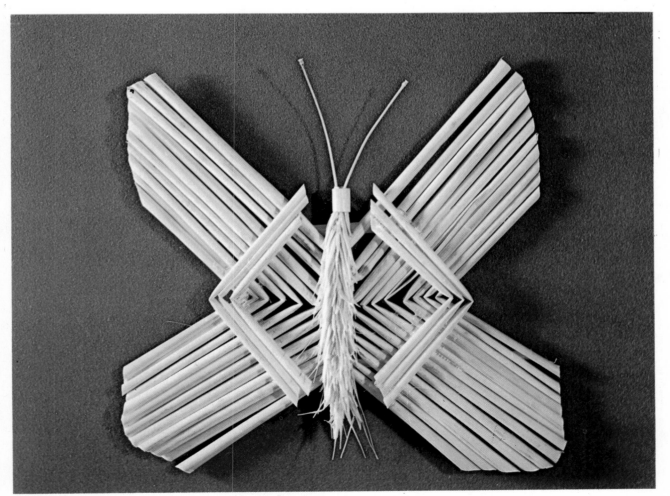

BOXES

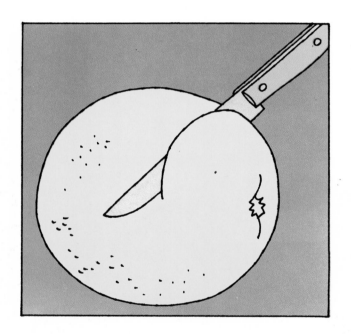

Cut the grapefruits or oranges into two parts, one much larger than the other.

Remove the pulp from the halves and clean them thoroughly, but do not remove the layer of white pith inside the skin.

Fit each skin over the bottom of a bottle to mold it into shape.
The bottle for the lower half should be slightly narrower than the one which forms the mold for the lid. This will insure that the lid fits neatly onto the box once the skins are dry.

Leave the skins to dry for several days on the molds, then remove them and make sure that they fit together properly. They can then be painted.
The finished boxes can be used to hold sweets, raisins or nuts when you have a party.

8

CANDLE HOLDER

To make this ornament you will have to find a suitably shaped piece of root or branch; it will need to have a solid base on one side and several vertical branches on the other.

Once you have found a root, work out the best position in which to mount it, then fix it to the board with nails or screws. This is slightly tricky, since you will have to hold the board in the air, or in a vice, while driving in the nails, so as not to damage the root.

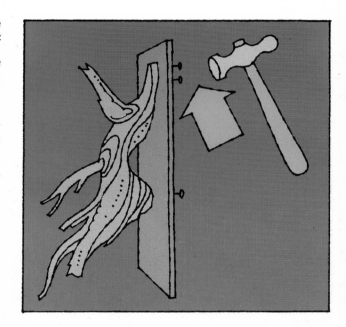

Once the candle holder is fixed onto the base, work out the heights at which the arms should be cut to make a balanced arrangement.

Cutting the arms also requires some care. The best method is to have someone hold the root down firmly on a table while you saw off the arms as shown. Make sure that their hands are kept well away from the saw.

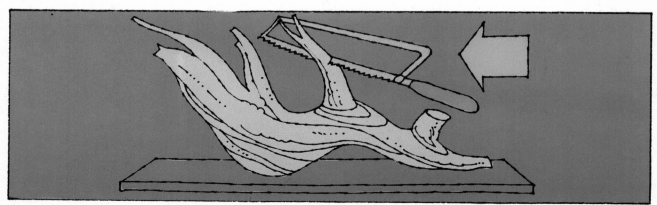

When the arms have been cut to length, they should be hollowed out slightly at the ends to take the candles. Use the tip of a sharp knife, as shown in the drawing.

The board on which the candle holder is mounted can be painted or left in its natural color.

Never leave a lighted candle burning in an empty room.

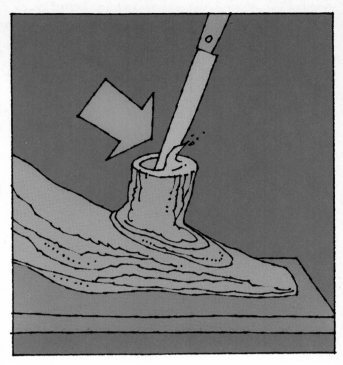

MATERIALS:
- Different kinds of corn or grass
- A wooden board
- Large pine cones
- A lump of clay
- PVA glue

TABLE PIECE

Place a lump of soft, damp clay in the middle of the board, then arrange the corn and grasses, sticking their stems into the clay.

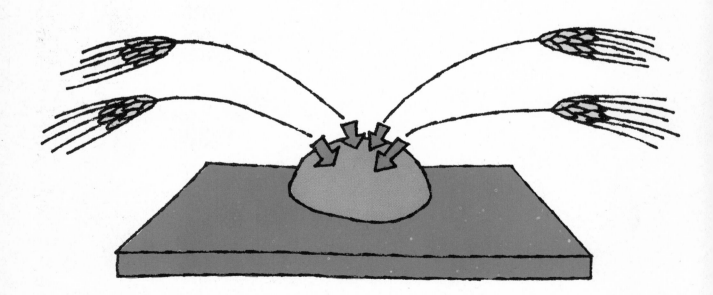

Arrange the cones around the clay so that they hide it, and fix them to the board with plenty of glue. When the clay dries out the stems will be firmly fixed.

The arrangement looks attractive in its natural colors. If preferred, the grasses can by dyed and the board and pine cones painted to obtain a more dramatic effect.

MOBILE

The body of each bird is made from an almond. A hazelnut is glued to the end of the almond as shown in the drawing, with the smooth, rounded side of the nut forming the bird's face.

Two colored glass beads are glued to the face to form the eyes; a short piece of quill, colored with an orange felt pen, forms the beak.

Feathers are stuck to each side of the bird as wings; a bunch of colored feathers at the back serves as a tail. Another feather can be stuck on top of the head as a crest.

The perches are made from wire, bent into shape with pliers. Each frame should have a hook at the top to hang the perch up by.

The wire should be flattened with a hammer at the points where the birds are glued in position. This will increase the area of metal in contact with the bird and make for a firmer fixing.

The perches and birds should be balanced carefully, so that the mobile hangs straight and moves in the slightest breeze.

Make a small indentation in the middle of the lower wire of each perch, as shown in the drawing. The hook of the perch beneath then fits into this and is prevented from sliding to and fro when the mobile is hanging freely.

Fix a ring to the hook of the topmost perch, so that the mobile can easily be hung from the ceiling or a tall piece of furniture.

MATERIALS:

- Walnut shells
- Toothpicks
- Leaves or paper
- Thin cane
- Wire and PVA glue
- Nylon thread
- Cellophane
- Paints

MOBILE

Cut out the sails from the leaves or paper. In this project we have used leaves from a sweet corn cob. Paint the toothpicks to make masts, and when the paint is dry, glue the sails onto them. Stick each mast to the bottom of a half walnut shell.

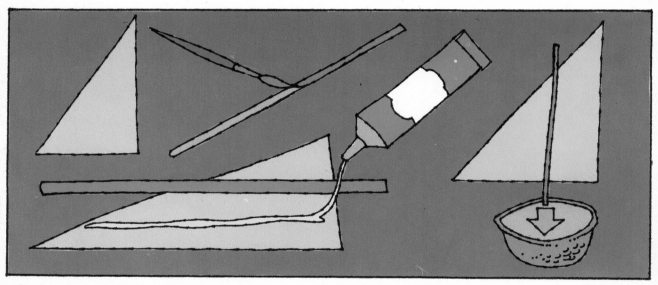

The cane frames are made as shown in the drawing. The corners are slotted together and glued.

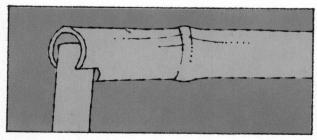

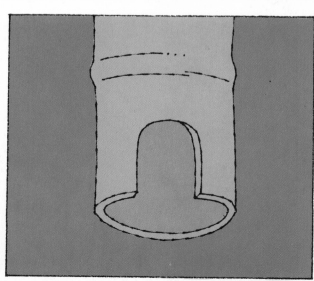

The upper cane of each frame should have several hollows made in it, to take the walnut shell boats. There should be one recess for each boat.

The cane frames are hung on wire hoops, which are bent at each end and fitted into the corner of the frame as shown. The wire hoops are then joined together with a length of nylon thread.

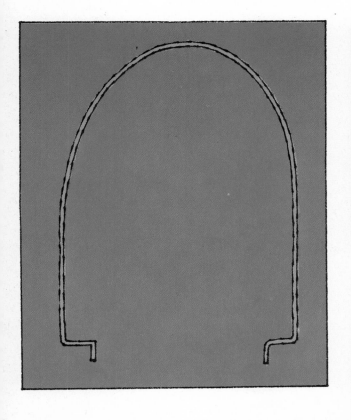

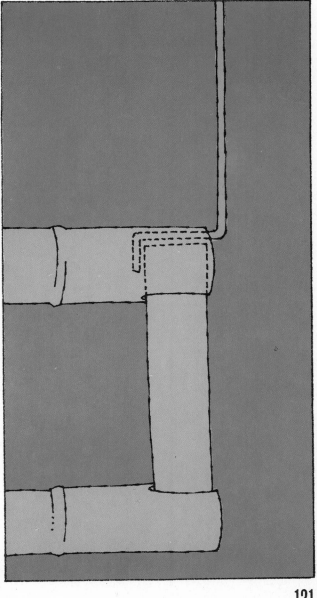

Cover the frames with blue cellophane and fix it to the frames with a little glue. Finally, glue each boat into its corresponding hollow.

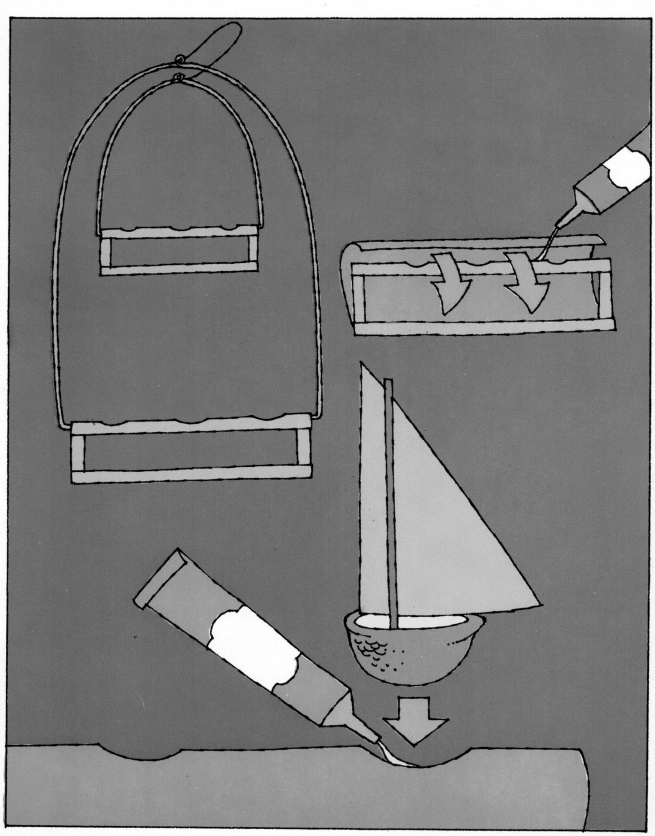

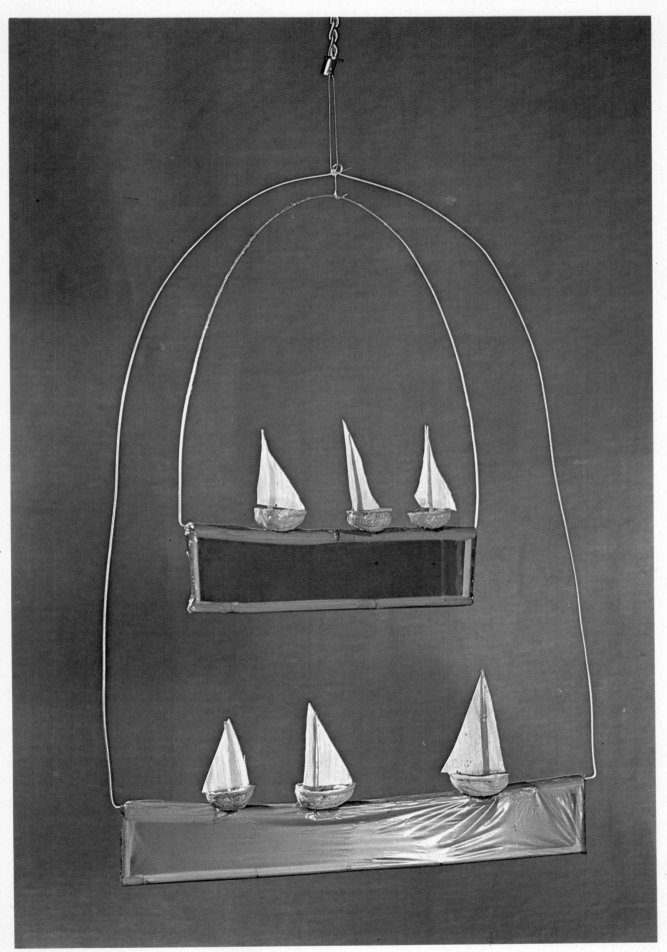

MATERIALS:

- Half a coconut shell
- A piece of cardboard
- Five long cones or curved twigs
- PVA glue
- Paints
- Plumber's hemp or wool
- Two red ribbons
- Knife, drill, needle and thread

MASK

Drill a hole in the center of the coconut shell to form the mouth.

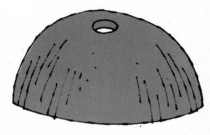

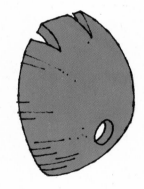

Now cut two slots in the top of the head, as shown in the drawing. These will serve to take the head-dress and the cord to hang the mask up by.

Cut a piece of cardboard the same shape as the shell, and glue a loop of cord onto it as shown. Fix the head decorations in the slots in the shell.
Stick the cardboard in position so that it covers the back of the shell. Use plenty of glue.

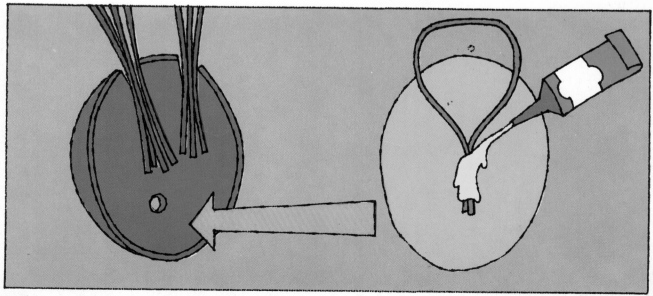

Take a bunch of plumber's hemp and sew several stitches through the middle to hold it together. If you find hemp difficult to get hold of you can use wool. Glue the hair onto the mask.

When the glue is dry, braid the hair at either end, and secure the ends with a bow of red ribbon.

Finally, paint in the eyes, nose and mouth.

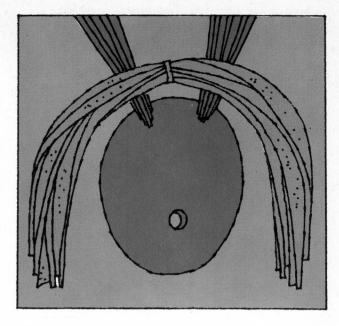

PENDANTS

Choose stones of a suitable size and color.
Give them a coat of varnish to bring out their natural colors.
Cut pieces of wire roughly twice the length required to cover the stones.

The extra length will be needed for the loops and twists. After a little practice with this kind of work, you will soon be able to judge by eye the length of wire needed for a particular stone.

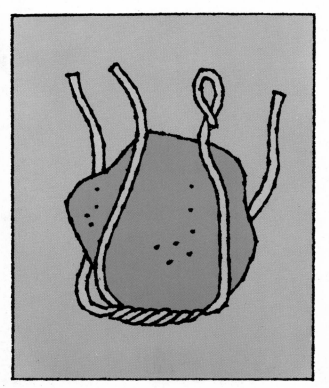

Use two wires for each stone. Twist them together as shown in the drawing. The four ends are then separated and wrapped around the stone so that they hold it firmly. Finally, join the wires in a loop at the top.

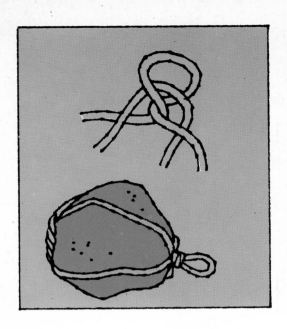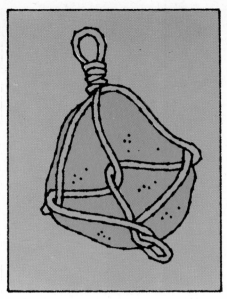

If the stone is to have a ring at both top and bottom, the wire should be looped around the stone as shown above right.
These stone pendants can be used in bracelets or necklaces or as ornaments for key rings.

NECKLACE

Give the stones a coat of clear varnish to bring out the colors.

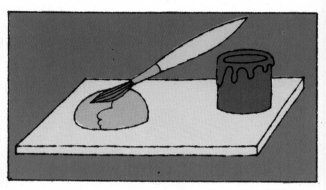

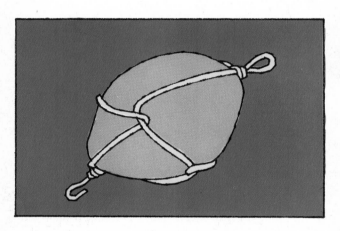

Cut some pieces of wire and loop them around the stones as shown in the drawing on the left. Make a small open hook at each end of the stones.

Once each stone is encased in wire, hook it onto the two chains, and close the hooks firmly around the link to which they are fixed; as the stones are relatively heavy there is some danger of the hooks opening with use and the necklace falling apart.

Hook the ends of the chain onto the two halves of the clasp.

The two chains should be of different lengths, the upper chain slightly shorter than the lower one. Find the length for each chain by trying the necklace on the wearer.

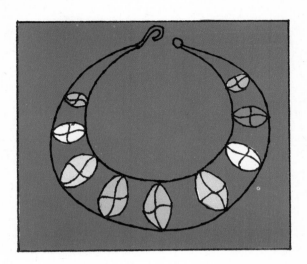

MATERIALS:
- Half a coconut
- A small pine cone
- A poppy seed head
- Two small lentils
- Colored feathers
- Four whole walnuts and four peanuts
- Paints
- PVA glue
- Sandpaper

HEN AND CHICKS

To make the hen, glue the pine cone which forms the neck onto one side of the coconut shell. Sandpaper the two surfaces flat so that they can be stuck together.

Stick the poppy seed head on top of the pine cone. The narrow end forms the beak. Glue a small piece of paper onto this to give it a point. The eyes are two lentils. Paint a circle of white around the edge of each eye, leaving the middle standing out in the natural color of the lentil.

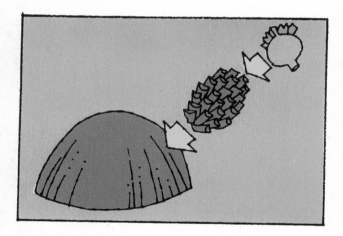

Fix a ruff of downy feathers around the base of the bird's neck.
Fasten a smaller ruff around the joint between the neck and head, and stick a crest in place with a drop of glue.
The wings are formed by two bands of down. Four feathers make up the tail. Pick out the beak with a dab of bright red paint.

SANDPAPER

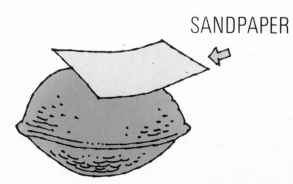

Make the body of each chick from a whole walnut. Sandpaper one side flat to make a base.

Glue a peanut to each walnut to form the head and neck.
You can use the small protrusion at one end of the shell to make the beak. Otherwise, make a beak from a scrap of paper. Add a small blue spot on either side for the eyes.

Finally, cover the whole walnut with glue and stick yellow down all over the chick's body.
The down can be trimmed to make it even.

The four chicks can be placed around the hen, or can even hide under her since they will fit very well beneath the half coconut shell.

MATERIALS:
- Wooden sticks
- Raffia
- A slice from a log of wood
- A piece of white card
- PVA glue

HUT

Cut a large number of sticks to the same length.
Pick out two long and fairly broad strands of raffia. Double them up and twist them around one of the sticks as shown in the drawing.

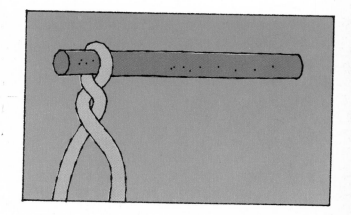

Join the remaining sticks together by twisting the raffia around them. This is quite easy, but it requires three people: one to hold the sticks which have already been joined, and the other two to twist the raffia around each new stick.

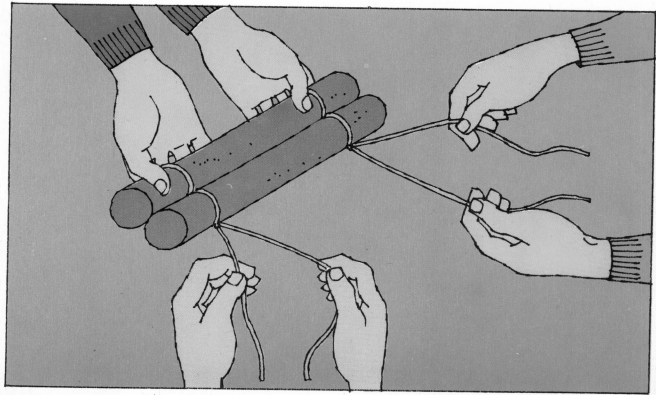

Alternatively, the first stick can be attached to a working surface so that only two people will be needed.

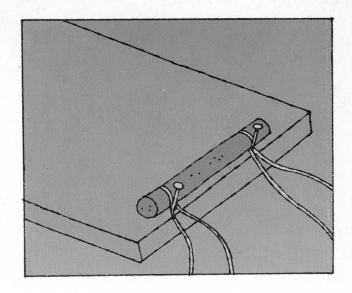

In either case, take care that the sticks are held tightly by the raffia and sit parallel to one another. If you run out of raffia before the job is completed, a new piece can easily be tied on.

Use shorter sticks for the doorway. You only need to use one strand of raffia but tie the sticks with great care. A drop of glue on each join will help to hold them in position.
When the hut is finished, glue it onto the log section which forms the base. Use plenty of glue so that the hut is stuck firmly in position.

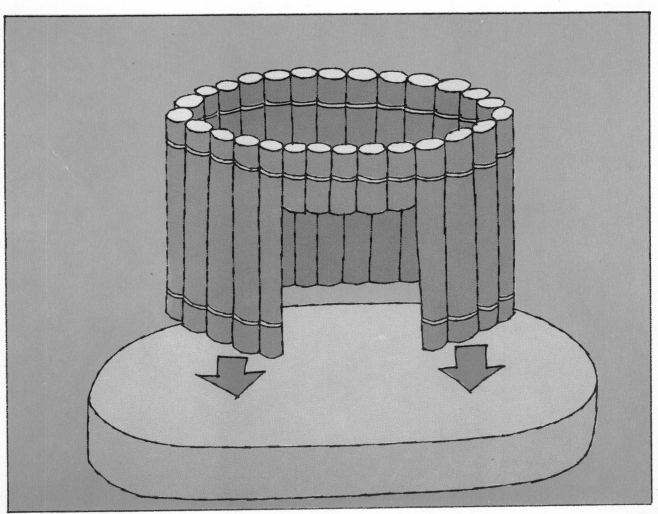

Cut a cone of white card, stick the edges together, and mount it on top of the hut.
Cover the card with glue and attach thick strands of raffia to form the thatched roof.

MATERIALS:
- Half a coconut shell
- Dried bean or seed pods
- Walnut shells
- Paints
- PVA glue

PORCUPINE

Smooth off the edges of the coconut shell so that it sits evenly on the ground. Paint the eyes and mouth as shown in the drawing.

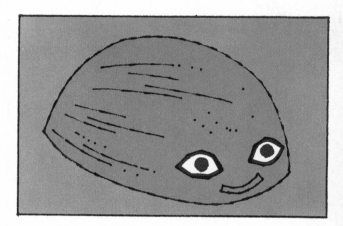

Glue sections of walnut shell around the edge to form the feet. Paint in the animal's claws.

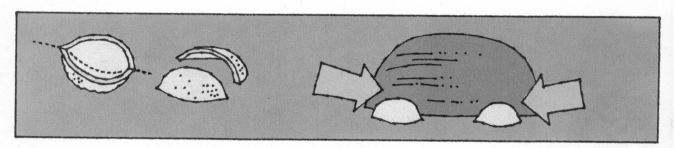

Cover the coconut shell with plenty of glue and stick on the seed pods, pressing them close together. These 'spines' should cover the whole of the body, leaving a small section at the front for the face.

MATERIALS:
- Small sticks and blocks of wood
- A thin board for the base
- Nylon thread
- PVA glue and a spring
- A cork which just fits inside the spring
- A vice and a chisel
- A bradawl or drill and paints

DOG

Cut and carve the different parts of the dog from the sticks and blocks of wood. You will need to make the head, collar, body, tail, two pieces for each leg and four paws. This project shows highly finished carving, but you can still make the dog with much simpler shapes.

Drill all the finished pieces as shown in the drawing. The holes can be made easily with a bradawl if the wood is green and tender.
If you are working with dry wood, the holes will have to be made with a proper drill.

In either case, take care not to injure your fingers. The best method is to fix the piece to be drilled in a vice, so that the fingers can be kept out of the way of the bradawl or drill.

When all the pieces are drilled, thread them onto the nylon thread as shown in the drawing.
Make four holes in the base board to take the four ends of the thread.
To make the base support, drill a hole through the middle of the square block of wood, then cut a recess on top slightly smaller than the base board. Use a chisel to cut the recess. The recess shown is a neat rectangle, but as the board will cover the recess it can be irregular in shape.

Make four holes in the side of the cork and cut a rectangle from the middle. Fit the cork into one end of the spring. Pass the ends of the thread through the four holes and knot them together. Depress the spring while doing this and adjust the length of the threads so that when the spring is released they will be drawn tight.

Insert the spring in the hole in the base support and glue the base board in position.

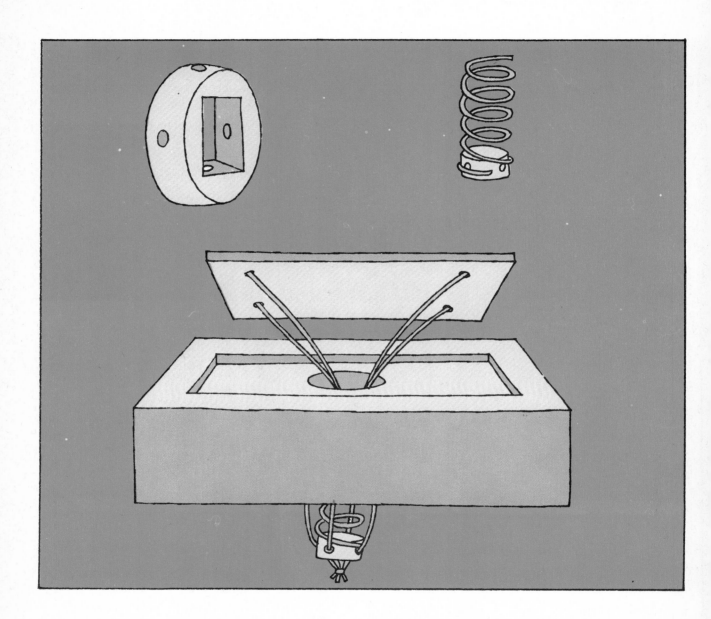

The dog and base can then be painted. If the dog's mechanism has been properly constructed, when the cork at the end of the spring is pressed from underneath the threads will slacken and the dog will collapse onto the base. When the spring is released the threads will tighten and the dog will leap upright again. With a little practice you can make it perform all kinds of amusing antics according to the way in which the spring is pressed.

If the dog does not work properly, try adjusting the thread to get the right tension.

MATERIALS:
● A small log
● Paints
● Pebbles
● PVA glue
● Clear varnish
● A small chisel and a mallet

PAINT BRUSH POT

Before starting work on the log, stand it up to see which end is more stable. Once you have decided which end is to be the base, draw a circle on the other end to indicate the area to be hollowed out.

The log should be fastened down securely while it is being worked on. Hold the chisel as shown in the drawing, with the bevel on the inside. Chisel around the pencil circle, then move the chisel to the middle of the circle and chip out the inside of the log, tapping gently with the mallet, and working from the middle out. Follow this method until you reach the required depth.

Then chip recesses in the side of the log to hold the stones.

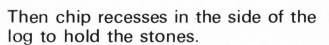

Next, paint the pot inside and out.

When the paint is completely dry, fix the stones in their places with a little glue.

STRAW WOMAN

Choose long, clean straws. It is best to use this material when it is still soft; if it is very dry, leave the straws in water for a few hours. Bend each straw in the middle, as shown in the drawing.

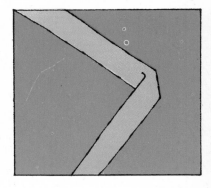

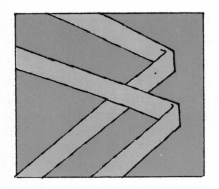

Start by laying the bent straws one on top of the other, as shown.

Leave one end of each straw free for the time being. Interweave the other end with the ends of the other straws.

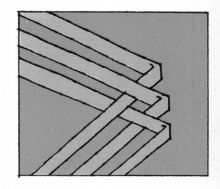

Continue adding straws in a row, as shown in the drawing. The folded centers of the straws will form the bottom edge of the work.

Bend a straw double and weave it in at the corner (see drawing, left).

Make the left-hand vertical edge by bending the straws over again as shown, until the strip is the required height.

Make the right-hand vertical edge by bending the straws over again, as you did for the left-hand edge.

Continue adding straws in a length-wise direction until the strip is long enough to form the base of the straw figure.

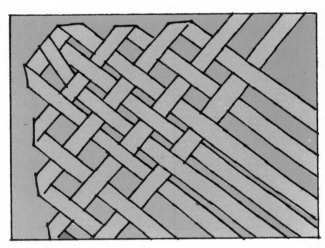

You will now have a strip with three straight edges, while on the fourth edge there will be a row of loose ends slanted to the right and another row slanted to the left. These ends should now be interwoven as shown in the drawing so that they stand vertically. The straws slanted to the right are looped through one another, starting from the right. The work is then turned over, and the same process is carried out with the row of straws which were slanted in the opposite direction.

10

Join the two ends of the strip together. The best method is to stitch them together with a length of straw.

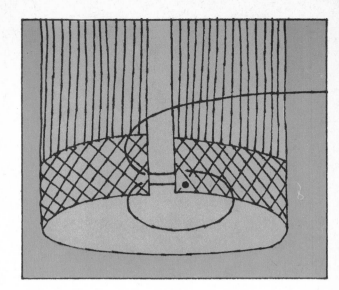

Gather the loose straws together and tie them with another straw to form the doll's waist.

Tie the sheaf again loosely a little farther up, then separate six or seven straws on each side and braid them to form the arms.

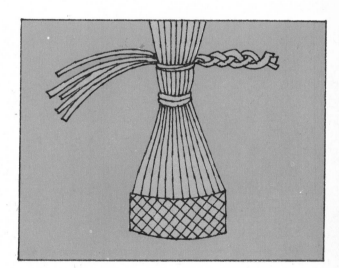

Tie the sheaf again at the neck, then bind it with another straw above the neck to form the face. The nose is formed by a single straw which is pulled from the sheaf and left outside the binding.

Split the ends left at the top of the head lengthwise into fine strands with a pair of scissors.
Bend them down around the face like flowing locks of hair.
Mark in the eyes, mouth and cheeks with dabs of paint.

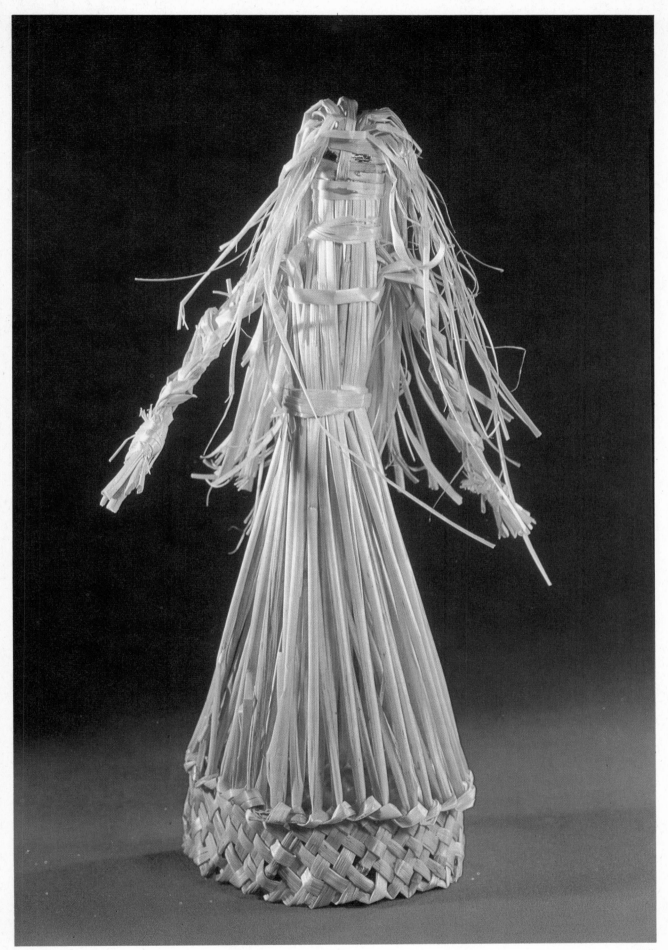

STOOL

Pick out the smoothest and most regular pieces of cane and assemble them in a row, as shown in the drawing. Nail them onto two cross pieces to form the seat of the stool. The canes should be strong enough to bear a person's weight.

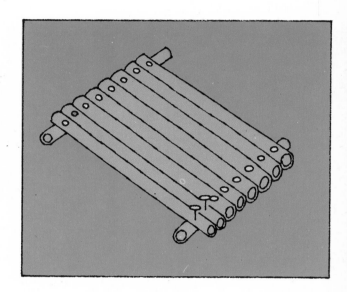

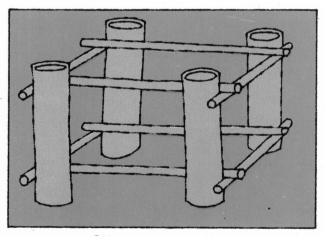

Four thicker lengths of cane form the legs; they should be exactly the same length so that the stool does not rock.

The four legs are joined by eight horizontal pieces, nailed in pairs to the inside and outside of each leg. Four diagonal struts will help to reinforce the legs. All these pieces should be nailed, glued and tied with string. It is essential that the base of the stool should be really firm, so that it does not collapse when someone sits on it.

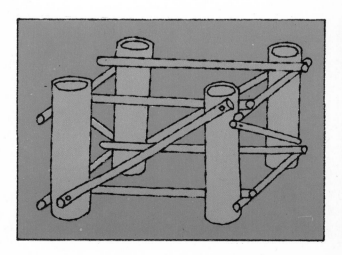

Fix the seat on top of the base. When the glue is dry and all the joints firmly nailed and tied, the stool can be used to support fairly light weights.

BIRD OF PARADISE

The basis of this bird is a piece of honeycomb, found on the ground during a country walk. You may have difficulty in finding a similar piece in such good condition, but if you can find some other material with an equally interesting pattern, such as a stone or a piece of bark, this will do just as well.

The bird's head and feet are carved from cuttlefish bone. This is very easy to work, but must be handled with care since it is rather brittle. Again, if you cannot find this material, use a flat piece of bone or wood.

Glue the body onto the velvet first, then add the head, the pine twigs and the feet.

The tail is made from colored feathers glued in position. The crest is another feather, separated into a number of points. The ruff is made by sticking several feathers around the join between the head and the body.
The finished picture can either be framed or pinned directly to the wall with drawing pins.

WIND GAUGE

Make a hole in the center of two walnut shell halves. Arrange the four sticks as shown in the drawing and glue them firmly to the edge of one of the halves.

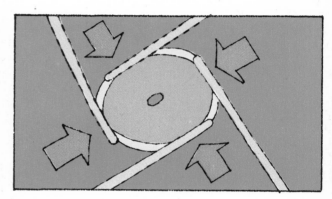

While the glue is drying, glue a fragment of shell over the hole in the other half to make a bearing for the spindle on which the gauge will be mounted.

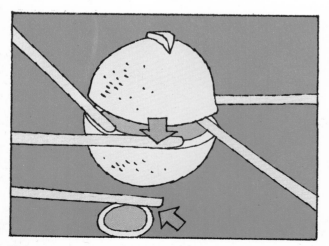

Stick the second half on top of the four sticks, again using plenty of glue. It is important that this joint should be really strong.

Glue a half walnut shell to the end of each stick, as shown in the bottom of the drawing.

Bend the wire so that it fits the shape of the stone and has a perfectly vertical stem rising from the center.

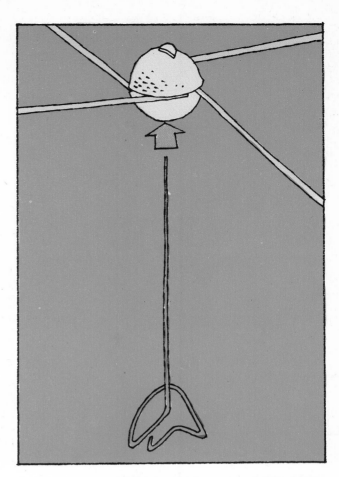

Fix the wire to the stone with plenty of glue. When the glue on all the joins is dry, the instrument can be assembled. Pass the vertical wire spindle through the holes in the central walnut shells so that the end sits in the bearing made for it.

As the wind blows against the concave shell at the end of each arm the vanes will turn, moving faster or slower according to the wind speed.

MATERIALS:
- Thin cane or reeds
- Paints

BASKETS

All the materials employed in basket work are easier to handle and less likely to break if they are well moistened before use.

ROUND BASKET

Select several long, thick pieces of cane to form the ribs of the basket.

Eight of these pieces should be arranged in a cross, as shown in the drawing. The point where they cross is the bottom of the basket.

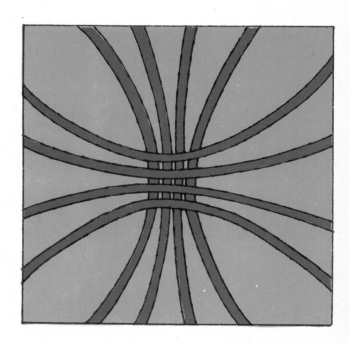

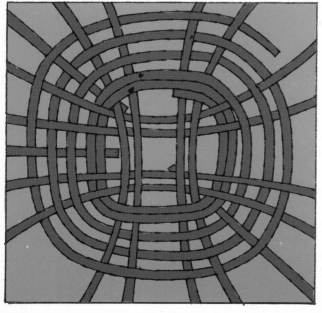

Now take a long piece of cane and start weaving it in and out around the eight ribs.

After weaving four full turns, add further ribs to make the segments through which the cane is woven as regular as possible. These additional ribs should be of an uneven number.

154

Once you have made the bottom of the basket, bend the ribs upwards and continue weaving vertically until you have achieved the right height.

During the course of weaving you will have to join on new pieces of cane a number of times. This is done by weaving the new piece parallel with the old piece for a short distance, let us say through six of the vertical ribs, as shown in the drawing.

To finish off the top edge of the basket, cut all the ribs to the same length. Then bend the end of each rib past the next rib and tuck it in beside the next but one. This will produce a looped pattern around the edge of the basket.

As the moistened cane dries out it will contract and the weave will become tighter and firmer.
The basket can be painted.

GONDOLA BASKET

Begin by choosing nine thickish pieces of cane for the ribs. Four of these are used to start with; the remaining five are added later.

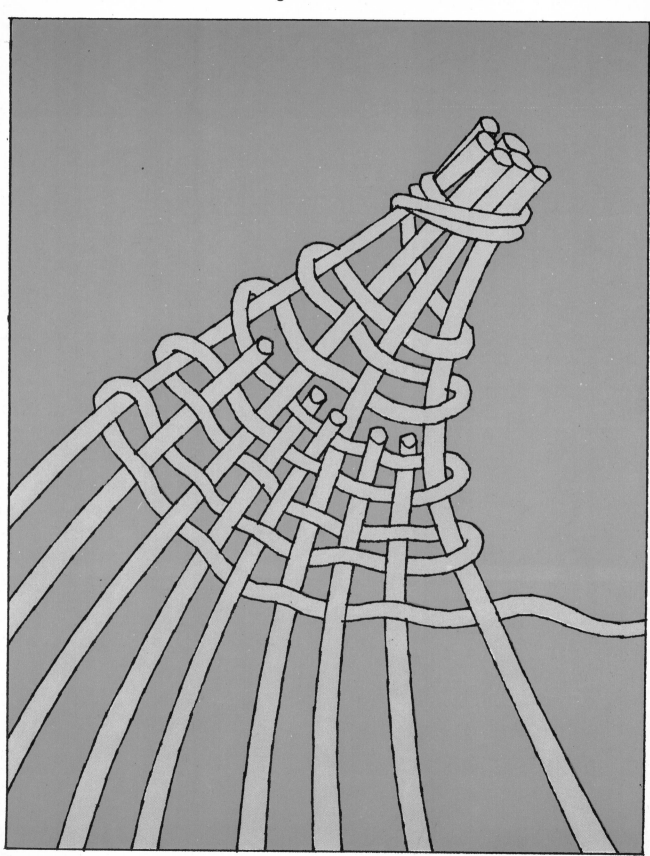

Bind the four ribs tightly at one end with a length of thin cane, and use this to start weaving. Press the weave down continually as you work or it will tend to spring apart.

After three or four rows have been woven, add the remaining five ribs as shown in the drawing.

Continue weaving, opening the ribs gradually so that the basket takes on its concave gondola shape.

When you reach the middle of the basket, reverse the process. Close the ribs gradually as you weave, and cut off the five ribs near the end. Finally, bind the remaining four with the piece of cane with which you have been weaving.

As with the round basket, it will be necessary to weave in new lengths of cane at regular intervals. This should be done by weaving the new piece alongside the old one for the space of several ribs.

FOSSILIZED FISH

Give the slate a coat of clear varnish. Before starting work with the graver, pencil in the design to be engraved.
Here we have used the form of a fish.

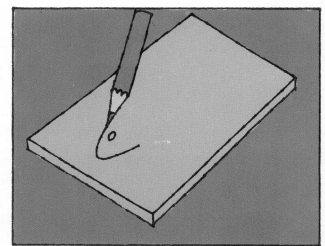

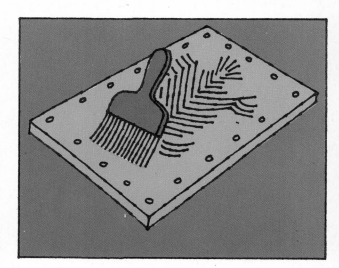

Engrave the design into the slate with any metal spike. Once the design is complete and all the lines have been engraved, clean off the slate dust with a soft brush.

The fish can be given a kind of frame if you engrave a row of dots around the edge of the slate and fill them in with white paint.

Fill in the outlines of the fish with white paint, using a fine brush. Wait until the paint is completely dry, then rub the slate hard with a rag to remove all trace of paint outside the engraved lines.

Make two holes in the upper edge of the slate with a bradawl. These will then take a cord to hang the picture up by.

The finished work looks very like a fossil.

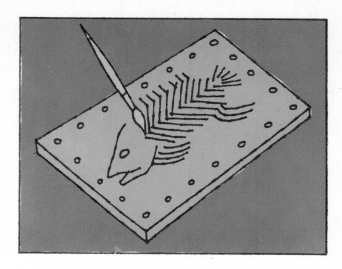

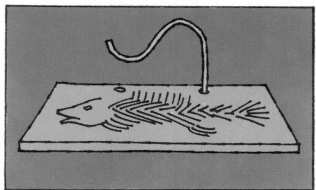

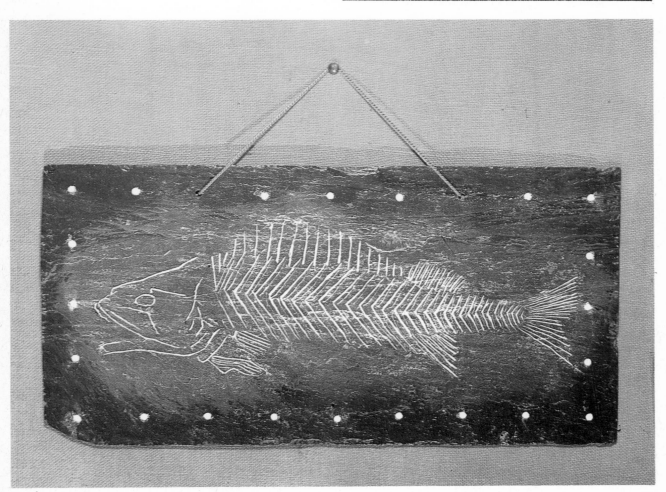

INDEX